SOUTH AFRICAN POLITICS
SINCE 1994

SOUTH AFRICAN POLITICS
SINCE 1994

Tom Lodge

DAVID PHILIP PUBLISHERS
Cape Town & Johannesburg

For Guy, Kim & Carla

First published 1999 in Southern Africa by David Philip Publishers
(Pty) Ltd, 208 Werdmuller Centre, Claremont 7708, South Africa

ISBN 0-86486-392-6

Map by James Mills-Hicks
Printed by Natal Witness

CONTENTS

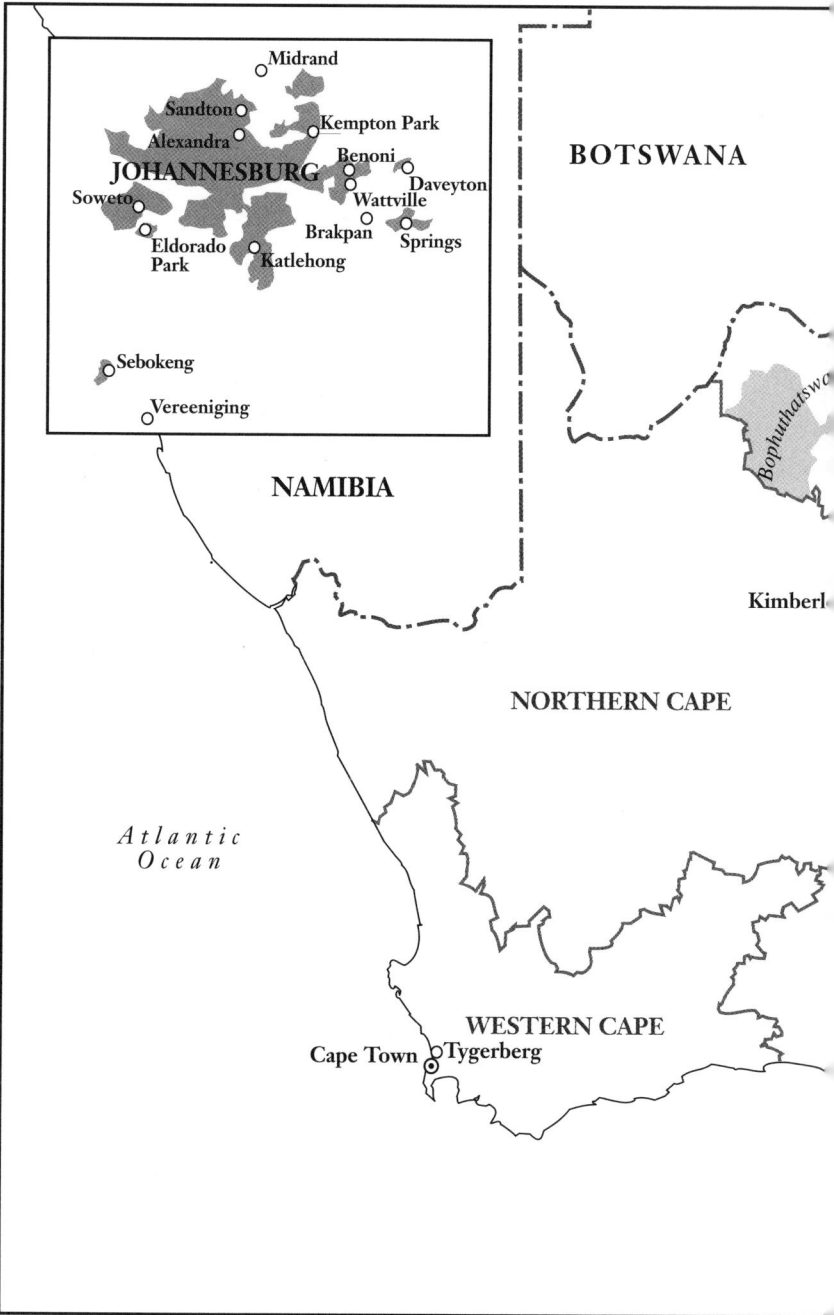

Midrand

Sandton

Kempton Park

Alexandra

Benoni

JOHANNESBURG

Daveyton

Soweto

Wattville

Brakpan

Springs

Eldorado
Park

Katlehong

Sebokeng

Vereeniging

BOTSWANA

Bophuthatswana

NAMIBIA

Kimberl

NORTHERN CAPE

Atlantic
Ocean

WESTERN CAPE

Cape Town

Tygerberg

Venda

MOZAMBIQUE

NORTHERN
PROVINCE Gazankulu

Lebowa

Pietersburg

Kgobokwane Bushbuckridge

KwaNdebele Dullstroom
Winterveldt Machadodorp
Pretoria Middelburg Nelspruit
GAUTENG Lochiel
eng Johannesburg Witbank Carolina

Leandra SWAZI-
see inset MPUMALANGA LAND

RTH
EST Sasolburg

Kroonstad

FREE STATE Qwa- Ulundi
Qwa

KWAZULU-
NATAL KwaZulu
mfontein

LESOTHO Pietermaritzburg

EC

Indian
Ocean

enstown

STERN CAPE Transkei

Bisho
Mdantsane East London
Ciskei
nhage

Port Elizabeth

N

W — E

S

⊙ Provincial capitals

former 'homelands' and
self-governing areas

0 200

km

ACKNOWLEDGEMENTS

I am indebted to my colleagues and students in the Department of Political Studies at the University of the Witwatersrand whose research on local government elections and local government performance I have drawn upon in Chapters 4 and 7. Both these research projects were funded by the Human Sciences Research Council, which also supports the Social Movement Project, findings from which are cited in Chapter 2. I am grateful to Media and Marketing Research, which allowed me access to the 1996 *Sowetan* Crime Survey mentioned in Chapter 5, and to the managers of the IDASA–SABC–EISA-Markinor survey, *Opinion 99*, to whose data I make reference in Chapters 2 and 6. An earlier version of Chapter 8 appeared in *Professional Management Review*. Many of the ideas and arguments in this book were tested in a series of lectures delivered to the University of Cape Town's Summer School of January 1998.

TOM LODGE

1

THE ALLIANCE IN POWER:
WHO RULES SOUTH AFRICA?

In the months which followed the April 1994 general election, African National Congress (ANC) leaders, struggling to come to grips with their new portfolios and ministries, often observed that there was a fundamental distinction between controlling the government and coming to power. The ANC, they said, was in government but it was by no means yet in power. 'Are we in power or merely in office?' asked Tokyo Sexwale, then premier of Gauteng, at a provincial ANC conference in November 1994, a refrain which also predominated in key addresses at the ANC's national conference that year. The ANC as the embodiment of 'the democratic majority . . . had won only some of the important elements of that political power necessary for the advancement of the struggle,' Deputy President Thabo Mbeki told the assembled delegates.[1]

The argument reflected, of course, the perception that the negotiated transition to democracy had required compromises – not the least of which was the acceptance of coalition partners. But at a more profound level, the distinction between government and power expressed a feeling that majoritarian democracy required something more than control of the executive and domination of representative institutions; that, moreover, while the state exhibited continuities with the pre-democratic bureaucracy the ANC's claim to be governing would be tenuous. Underlying these considerations was the belief, deeply entrenched not just in the political-activist community but also influencing much of the political analysis generated from academic institutions, that power

– real power – was invested somewhere other than in government.

In this book I intend to qualify this picture. Of course, political power is not a state monopoly, and it is not confined to parliament, cabinet, officialdom, party leadership and so forth. I am, however, going to argue that what the ANC likes to call, in referring to the 1994 election, 'the democratic breakthrough' did indeed signify a profound change in the distribution and shape of power relations in South Africa. The distinction between government and political power is not a simple one. The two are not synonymous – but neither are they separate. In this discussion, I want to begin to look at the political complexities brought about by the 'democratic breakthrough' by trying to answer the question Who rules South Africa?

The ANC's victory at the polls was not just the triumph of a political party. Rather it signified the political supremacy of a broader liberatory movement whose constituents included the ANC itself – an organisation which until its legalisation and homecoming in 1990 had been constituted by a 15,000-strong exile body largely, though not exclusively, oriented to guerrilla warfare, and which by 1991 had built a branch structure inside South Africa embracing a membership of 500,000.[2] Another vital part of the movement was the Congress of South African Trade Unions (COSATU) labour federation, with an affiliate strength in 1994 of 1.2 million members. The South African National Civic Organisation (SANCO), the national civic movement, helped to embody the legacy of the lively localised tradition of community politics which had been led by the United Democratic Front (UDF) during the 1980s. A rapidly growing Communist Party (SACP) included in its leadership a substantial share, though not all, of the ANC's leaders and much of the movement's intelligentsia.

The liberation movement was a social alliance, given formal expression by the relationship between these different formations. An alliance between the ANC and the SACP had existed since the establishment of Umkhonto weSizwe (MK) in 1961 and the subsequent formation of a Revolutionary Council on which members of both organisations served. COSATU, formed in 1985, had by 1987 adopted the ANC's Freedom Charter (though not without misgivings among some of its more left-wing officials). The civic movement and other constituents of the Mass Democratic Movement (a formation which brought together in 1989 trade unions, the UDF and certain churches in a Defiance Campaign) was also aligned with the ANC when that organisation began reconstructing itself inside South Africa, though the civics have never enjoyed the same status as Alliance partners in ANC circles as have the labour movement and the SACP. COSATU's status as the ANC's labour ally was confirmed by the decision taken in 1990 to transfer to the federation the assets of the old exile union centre, the South African Congress of Trade Unions (SACTU), then undergoing dissolution. In June 1990 COSATU–ANC workshops were held in Harare to plan policies for a post-apartheid government.

Despite these early affirmations of accord, the next few years would witness evidence of rising tensions between the ANC's leadership and trade unionists. The latter complained of ANC 'unilateralism' in its decision to suspend guerrilla war in August 1990 and in its advocacy at the beginning of 1991 of an all-party congress that should negotiate the route to a constituent assembly. For a while, trade unionists demanded a separate delegation at any such negotiations, and indeed they drew up a separate set of constitutional provisions. These included proportional representation and a presidency limited to two terms, both features of today's Constitution which did not appear in early ANC constitutional proposals. COSATU was to drop its demand for separate representation but its spokesmen continued to display considerable independence as well as impatience at any conciliatory predisposition they perceived among ANC negotiators towards the government. They also became increasingly resentful of the ANC's tendency to substitute negotiation for mobilisation as well as the exploitation of mobilisation as a merely auxiliary tactic to create a public resonance for the arguments used by negotiators. From 1993, however, senior trade unionists began to invest their political efforts in elaborating the ingredients of a 'reconstruction accord', a pact which would supply the basis for an ANC election manifesto and would constitute the condition for COSATU's support during the poll.

The genesis of the Reconstruction and Development Programme (RDP) stemmed from this tacit bargain between the ANC's leadership and COSATU. The RDP's first four drafts were chiefly the product of policy expertise associated with the trade union movement. Three further drafts were debated at meetings which built up a wider range of consensus between the ANC, the trade unions, the SACP, Mass Democratic Movement affiliates and a range of sectoral non-governmental organisations (NGOs). The key COSATU planners involved in drafting the programme in its early stages were Alec Erwin, Jay Naidoo, and Bernie Fanaroff. As the RDP evolved, its contents drew upon an increasingly broad diversity of tributaries. Since 1990 the ANC itself had moved a considerable distance away from its traditional *dirigiste* preoccupations. In 1990 the ANC–COSATU workshop in Harare had embraced a set of proposals which would have included an extension of public ownership, state regulation of credit, a prescribed high-wage economy, and a central role for organised labour in policy formulation. Redistribution would serve as the principal agency of economic growth.

Through 1991, though, ANC economists began to shift ground. The 1992 Draft Policy Guidelines included the suggestion that the public sector might need to be reduced, they noted the necessity for legal protection of property rights, and they reflected an increased sensitivity to the requirements of international competition for South African manufacturing.[3] Later critics of ANC policy-making suggested that 'top ANC economic staffers', including the then policy principals, Tito Mboweni and Trevor Manuel, had been intellectually corrupted by their participation in private sector think-tanks, training courses, scenario building exercises, and social encounters with officials from the World Bank.[4]

The RDP reflected both the earlier and the later economic predispositions within the ANC as well as other discourses. Some 41 pages out of a total of 147[5] addressed economic concerns. Its argument opened with an acknowledgement that the South African economy was characterised by 'deep structural crisis', including unproductive manufacturing, inefficient labour, over-subsidised agriculture, a growing government deficit and an exodus of private capital. Remedies should include unbundling and deracialising corporate ownership, a strategic role for the public sector – which might have to be either enlarged or reduced (the ambiguity reflected conflicting imperatives for the drafters) – a 'living wage' and training for workers, the removal of subsidies from unproductive enterprises, land reform and fiscal restraint. Development projects should involve and 'empower' ordinary people, and should be the outcome of popular initiatives and wide-ranging 'people-driven' consultations. Economic growth would be substantially boosted by the expansion of consumer demand; this would follow the construction of huge numbers of cheap houses and the extension to poor people of electrical and piped water supplies. In its final form, the RDP represented a careful balance between the 'growth through redistribution' policies advocated by the left and the emphasis on growth as the harbinger of redistribution in more orthodox economic analysis. As such it certainly reflected the ANC's engagement with an increasingly diverse range of social actors in the four years which had elapsed since its homecoming.

So, who has ruled South Africa since the ANC's accession to power? Big business complains about a government which they perceive, or claim to perceive, as acting in tandem with the interests of organised labour. COSATU – and some communists – agree that democracy has been hijacked by the representatives of international capital, who have succeeded in corralling the ANC within the hegemonic confines of 'neo-liberal' economics. *Vox populi* opinion recorded on radio talk shows or in newspaper correspondence columns suggests widespread popular disenchantment with, alternatively, a replication of previous hierarchies of privilege or, conversely, a mean-spirited racial antagonism directed at white South Africans. Opinion polls, on the other hand, indicate modest expectations and a degree of satisfaction with the government's performance.[6] What is one to make of all this?

None of these sentiments accord much recognition to the possibility that politics follows its own course, that command of the state certainly invests the governing class with considerable social autonomy – but an autonomy which is also constrained by social actors, by ideology and moral beliefs, and by perceptions of the possible. I do believe this. Part of my conviction stems, no doubt, from my own sympathies and preferences. The ANC leaders I have met seem likeable and impressive and I find it hard to regard people who in the past made such costly personal sacrifices, as servants of selfish or sectional concerns. But aside from such sentiment, there are more analytical grounds for taking their independence as politicians seriously, for they control a state which in comparative terms – when considered alongside the bureaucracies of other comparable developing countries – is strong, efficient and powerful.[7] For example, foreign public debt is unusually low, which makes South African financial policy-makers much less susceptible to monetarist pressure from international lending agencies.[8] The managers of public finance do not need to serve other masters than those they profess loyalty to.

Who influences the state? is a better question than Who rules it. First of all, what is the political significance of the Alliance? Have the years since 1994 witnessed 'the Alliance in power' as the title of this chapter suggests? Not if you take seriously the angry rhetoric which COSATU's leadership have directed at the government and especially at the macroeconomic measures embodied in GEAR, the Growth, Employment and Redistribution strategy, with their emphasis on deficit reduction, government 'rightsizing', tariff reduction, privatisation, and productivity-linked wage rates. GEAR was drafted secretly and presented to the ANC's National Executive in mid-1996 as a *fait accompli*. As an exasperated COSATU discussion paper noted at the end of the year, when it comes to making policy 'the Alliance engaged only with the product'.[9]

The debates over GEAR, though, have tended to divert attention away from those areas in which labour has made solid gains, often despite intense opposition from business circles. Labour legislation is an obvious case in point both with reference to the

Industrial Relations Act of 1995 and to the more recent Basic Conditions of Employment law. To be sure, labour may have appeared to lose on symbolic issues – the constitutional status of lock-outs or the forty-hour week are examples – but there can be no question that trade unions have been significantly fortified by legal changes since 1994. Trade unionists might respond that such gains are illusory in a situation of shrinking employment (businessmen claim that unemployment is accelerated by these labour reforms as investors seek more 'flexible' labour markets elsewhere), but compared with other national economies under-going economic 'restructuring', the fall in formal employment in South Africa (100,000 in 1997) has been comparatively mild (with public sector jobs not decreasing at all), and wages have actually risen in real terms. Official statistics released in October 1998 suggested that in non-farm employment, the number of new jobs (289,108) roughly balanced the number of jobs lost (278,901) between 1994 and 1998. Agriculture, forestry and fish-ing between 1995 and 1996 had lost 815,000 existing jobs while only a small number of new jobs were created.[10] So in those sec-tors which have been most strongly organised by trade unions, employment levels have been fairly stable.

Organised labour can also derive satisfaction from the slow pace of privatisation and their own success in helping to define its process. Arguably, broader access to health care, increased pub-lic expenditure on education, and the efforts to reform social welfare all represent a significant expansion of the social wage. Again, as with rises in real wages, this expansion runs against international trends. What is true, though, is that such policies have seldom reflected a systematic joint process of strategic direc-tion by the ANC and its partners. The various Alliance summits and conferences, when they have been held at all, have usually been occasions when ministers and other members of the gov-ernment have been taken to task for the shortcomings of policies already under implementation. As COSATU observed in December 1996, 'the locus of decision-making on key political issues has not been in Alliance structures but in individual min-istries'.[11] Nor has the SACP, despite the conspicuous role that some of its members play in government (4 cabinet ministers, 2 provincial premiers and 53 MPs),[12] shown any more evidence of exercising a corporate influence, not least because of the divisions within the party elite, which have widened since the paradigmatic rupture that accompanied the demise of East European communism.

Moving away from the formalised structure of the Alliance, with what justification can Nelson Mandela and his colleagues claim to be a 'people's government'? There was, initially, considerable effort invested in participatory development procedures in which local projects such as water reticulation or housing construction or improving local roads would be inspired and managed by locally representative bodies. The RDP's adoption was accompanied by the assembly of hundreds of local development forums which were supposed to function in partnership with state agencies in conceiving and funding such projects.

Some of these forums survive, but project implementation has mostly been a top-down affair, partly because of the difficulty in achieving consensus in divided communities, partly also as a consequence of the requirements of scale and speed. We will be discussing RDP programmes with these considerations in mind later in this book. The absence of responsive and legitimate local government until its election in 1995 and 1996 also posed an obstacle for the 'people-driven' progress of the RDP. In addition, the ANC's own lack of preparation for municipal politics meant that even after their entry into town halls many ANC councillors have been ineffectual (and often corrupt as well).

In its rhetoric, the ANC invests great faith in its own internal democratic procedures, and since its conference in Mafikeng in December 1997, it is committed to revitalising these. But the ANC's claim to embody 'a parliament of the people' needs to be understood in a context in which paid-up membership has halved since the 1994 election and in a situation in which thousands of its most effective organisers have found employment in legislatures and government, considerably distanced from the communities they used to mobilise so successfully. The latest revisions to the ANC's constitution have extended the interval between national conferences from three to five years, effectively limiting the prospects that the organisation's leadership might become more accountable to its membership and its more inchoate popular following.[13]

What about big business? Like trade unionists, local business-men – at least in public – exaggerate the gulf which separates them from government. One should try to distinguish the general interest of business from more specific concerns. Revision of protective import tariffs, for example, is not a measure which finds unanimous favour among South African business circles. Certain business sectors have encountered especially hostile attitudes from government departments and their political leadership – the relationships between the Department of Health and the pharmaceutical and tobacco industries would be two cases in point – whereas others have experienced more sympathetic predispositions. Gambling and liquor are two industries which have developed sophisticated and successful lobbying strategies, with respect both to parliament and to individual ministries.

In general terms, the government has probably been better for business than any of its predecessors for a very long time – labour reforms notwithstanding – not so much through any direct assistance to business, though corporate taxation remains restrained, but rather through its evident acceptance of what businessmen perceive to be economic common sense, with respect to public expenditure levels, exchange control and foreign trade. But this is different from being a government wedded to the interests of the private sector, even supposing that those could ever be encapsulated neatly by policy. Rhetoric at the 1997 Mafikeng conference about the need to make business more 'socially accountable' should be taken seriously, particularly with respect to job creation.

Though the pace of deracialisation of ownership has been quite swift – 'black-chip shares' as a proportion of the total market capitalisation on the Johannesburg Stock Exchange have grown from 0.05 per cent in 1995 to almost 20 per cent in 1998[14] – government leaders still perceive business as representing a different constituency from their own.[15] This helps to maintain a social distance between the government and business which makes it unlikely that government will be particularly sensitive to every anxiety within the business community, particularly those which trouble local capitalists. Amongst the ANC's 252 MPs, only a small number, 32, have registered shareholdings worth more than R10,000, and 20 maintain directorships, though many of these are unremunerated commitments to NGOs.[16]

There are indications, though, that this gulf between ruling party politicians and business may become narrower in the near future. In late 1997, the ex-ANC Youth Leaguer, hair-salon chain director, and deputy minister of tourism, Peter Mokaba, circulated a pre-conference discussion paper which suggested that 'the Freedom Charter [had] always aimed to build a capitalist South Africa'. The ANC should make its priority, Mokaba urged, 'a process that builds the black section of the entrepreneurial class'.[17] Mokaba also challenged the privileged position that the SACP enjoyed within the tripartite Alliance, referring to communists 'who sit in ANC meetings' and who then 'convene under another name and criticise decisions they took as the ANC'.[18] Mbeki's and Mandela's rebukes to COSATU and SACP in June 1998 for their criticisms of the government's macroeconomic policy reflected the same vein of irritation. These were followed by Thabo Mbeki's condemnation of 'traitors' and 'criminals' in the South African Democratic Teachers' Union,[19] and the strictures of the minister of constitutional development, Valli Moosa, against 'ultraleftist' agitation among municipal workers against privatisation.[20] Meanwhile, Cyril Ramaphosa, in his capacity as the South African Breweries (SAB) acting chairman, warned in his annual report that the 'recent procession of labour enactments' could be 'cost burdensome' and so could inhibit job creation.[21] A further signal of the ANC's move away from its traditional ideological moorings was the angry dismissal by the minister of agriculture, Derek Hanekom, of the National Land Committee's proposal for the scrapping of the constitutional property clause as 'stubborn frivolousness'.[22]

What about the government itself? Do its leadership and managers represent a class in the making, a bureaucratic bourgeoisie of the kind familiar to most observers of nationalist movements which came to power elsewhere on the continent? I do not think so. Blocking this development are several barriers; these include the continuities from the old regime (this is not a decolonised public service), the egalitarian traditions which still form such an important part of the ANC's intellectual constitution, the general trajectory of state development in the 1990s in which the state's role in the economy decreases rather than expands, and the existence of a strong workers' movement as a component of the liberatory alliance. Chapter 5 specifically addresses the topic of political corruption, but it is worth observing here how limited its incidence is among elected office-holders, compared with its extensiveness within the civil service. A final barrier to the emergence of a bureaucratic bourgeoisie is the strange resilience of liberal institutions in South Africa, some nurtured by liberation politics, others independent and even in opposition to them. Chapter 6 develops and elaborates this argument further.

So the answer to my question Who rules South Africa? is both obvious and deceptive. A political movement governs – and has real power, as we shall see, to reshape political and economic life. The interests its represents are amorphous – the constituents of a social alliance: organised labour, black entrepreneurs, an emergent managerial class, rural poor, a multiracial intelligentsia informed by competing humanitarian and radical traditions. No one group is dominant nor is the likely ascendancy of any one of these certain. They struggle for influence in a relatively poor, middle-income, developing country on the margins of the international economy, or, from a different perspective, on the borders of what separates the rich industrial world from the desolation of what Frantz Fanon called the 'wretched of the earth'. In such uncertain territory no social group holds undisputed power.

2

REGIONAL GOVERNMENT

Most government in the new South Africa is regional. The regional administrations established in 1994 spend about two-thirds of the national budget and employ the vast majority of the country's 1.2 million public servants. Some 400,000 of these are the former functionaries of the old apartheid 'homelands', or putatively self-governing black territories which became labour reservoirs for white South Africa. Regional governments are responsible for those aspects of administration which affect the everyday life of citizenry: health, pension payments, education, housing. When people give judgments about the government's success in making a better life for them they are evaluating, mainly, the performance of regional administrations. Regional governments do not have much discretion in determining policy – the laws they pass in most domains have to conform with the principles underlying policies determined by central government – but they have considerable latitude in interpreting policy and implementing it. Their capacities are also limited by their lack of any significant source of independent finance – their budgets are allocated from central government – but disbursement of such funds gives their politicians considerable real power, nevertheless. No adequate analysis of modern South African politics can overlook the way these administrations operate.

The establishment of nine regional polities owed much to the imperatives of a negotiated transition to democracy in which the ANC was persuaded of the wisdom of making concessions to smaller parties. The case for South African democracy's assuming a federal form was based chiefly on the supposed political benefits of a multi-centred political dispensation in ethnically divided societies. Dividing executive authority between central and regional government would give minorities, defined in different ways, a stake in the system. In a post-nationalist politics characterised by a dominant majority party, federal or regional devolution of power held out to small parties, with no hope of winning office at the centre, the prospect of achieving executive control at subordinate levels. Federal governments also protect local or regional interests against big central government. Less conspicuous in the South African advocacy of the merits of federalism was the possibility that it could bring government closer to citizenry, making it more accessible and accountable; and that the devolution of power might enhance democracy, allowing small communities more capacity to influence or determine the behaviour of politicians. Notably absent, though, from any of the South African motivations for regionalised constitutions were any arguments about efficiency or developmental benefits.

In this chapter, I want to explore the effects of regional government. I am going to look at three separate dimensions of their existence. Firstly, I want to examine the quality of their public administration. Secondly, I would like to consider the politics of regionalism, especially its effect on party politics. Because I will be looking at the northern provinces as case studies, I will be concerned chiefly with the ANC. Finally, I want to discuss the ways in which provincial governments are regarded by ordinary people. Have they, as the exponents of federalism maintain they should, enhanced the legitimacy of government?

Firstly, we deal with administration. When things go wrong in South African government, more often than not they go wrong in the regions. This is not altogether surprising. Several of the regions on their inception were confronted with the task of amalgamating several separate civil services from the old white provincial bureaucracies, whatever administrative arrangements may have existed for Indians and coloured people, and the former homelands, each of which had developed their own managerial styles and most of which lacked technical skills and professional integrity. The new boundaries also brought together competing or rival political elites often very jealous of each other's influence. The tensions in the Eastern Cape between Transkeian ANC supporters of an additional 'tenth region' and the more senior political leadership based in Mdantsane (outside East London) and in Port Elizabeth would be a case in point. They inherited administrations in which bureaucratic systems had broken down or disappeared. They lacked accurate and reliable information about the identities and numbers of employees and the accounting of public expenditure for over a decade. In the Transkei, for example, government accounts were last audited in 1988. They did not have basic information about the quality and even the location of government facilities – offices, buildings and the equipment they may have contained.

Not surprisingly, those provinces which have since 1994 acquired a reputation for relatively efficient performance of services – Gauteng, Western Cape, Northern Cape and the Free State – are those which have been least encumbered with the legacies of homeland administrations. In the case of Gauteng, the bureaucracy was reconstructed anew because the decision to base its administrative centre in Johannesburg rather than Pretoria meant that it did not have to assemble itself around the old Transvaal Provincial Administration (many of whose members were reluctant to make the move between the two cities and so opted for early retirement). The new regional government of Gauteng could draw its recruits from the public service training institutions concentrated on the Witwatersrand.

Some of the difficulties, then, which regional administrations have experienced are attributable to shortages of technical or professional skills. In the Northern Province, for example, of 290 doctors employed in public hospitals in 1996 – itself a woefully inadequate total for a population of about six million – only 20 were South African citizens; the rest were foreigners. Not that the Northern Province's public service is generally undermanned: it employs one-third more people than the considerably more populous Gauteng. Even Gauteng, though, suffers from a shortage of properly qualified accountants: departmental budgets of R1 billion are supervised by people with basic bookkeeping skills. In the Eastern Cape and KwaZulu-Natal, schools are especially handicapped by under-qualified teachers – and tens of thousands of teachers on their payrolls do not exist at all. The absence of effective control systems encouraged fraud and waste – bad habits which have been around for a very long time and which only now have come to light. In one northern district of KwaZulu–Natal it was discovered in 1996 that 97 per cent of the local population were supposedly receiving disability allowances. The crisis in pension pay-outs in the Eastern Cape during 1997 was mainly caused by the delays arising from the reorganisation of a pension system in which huge sums of money were paid to fictional claimants. A provincial audit concluded that over the next ten years 22,000 qualified personnel would have to be recruited annually to make up the province's skills deficit.

Central government has attempted to address these problems by discriminating against the richer or better-resourced provinces in budgetary allocations, Gauteng and the Western Cape in particular. This caused the two provinces to overrun their budgets in health and education in 1997. Increased funding to poorer provinces, though, has only accentuated their administrative difficulties: they lack the capacity to spend money efficiently. The skills which are concentrated in the urbanised provinces do not follow the redirection of public funding: teachers and health professionals and technical staff move instead into the private sector. The facilities which are most affected by this exodus or budgetary cuts are, of course, most likely to be located in the poorest communities – Baragwanath Hospital in southern Johannesburg is a case in point.

I do not want to spend too much time, however, on administrative problems. I am not sure, in any case, that the overall quality of regional government is much worse than what it replaced, and in certain respects it may be better. Opinion polls suggest that people in poor rural areas believe they now enjoy better access to government services such as health facilities.[23] Some of the reports of administrative strain, especially in the health services, are entirely attributable to the fact that more people are making claims on government. I now want to turn to a consideration of the political dimensions of the new federal order.

Federal politics has vastly increased the complexity for the ANC of running its own inner organisational life. Between 1994 and 1998, in the seven ANC-governed provinces there have been three changes of premiership – two of them, in Gauteng and the Free State, sharply contested. In most of the provinces there have been conflicts between ANC people in government and their respective party leaderships, especially in those instances in which the premiership and the party chairmanship have been held by different people. Political corruption in the strict sense of venality amongst elected politicians has been most evident in provincial administrations, notably in Mpumalanga. Rank and file rebellions against the efforts of national leadership to influence the outcome of regional leadership contests have arisen in Gauteng, the Northern Province and the Free State. Provincial premiers have been demonstrably keen to extend the boundaries of their autonomy in policy matters. Tokyo Sexwale's efforts to develop an independent (and very expensive) housing programme with a private construction firm, Stocks & Stocks, was an early instance of this. Mathews Phosa's efforts as Mpumalanga's premier to conduct a provincial foreign policy with neighbouring Mozambique would be another example.

Some of the difficulties can be explained by the ANC's organisational character in the provinces, where it is often a disparate and awkward sum of its parts. The ANC between 1990 and 1994 expanded its organised following very rapidly and in doing so incorporated a multitude of different local political cultures as well as contrasting styles of political leadership. This was an especially obvious feature of rural provinces, in which governments reflected uneasy coalitions of old-style homeland bosses, veterans of the militant and militaristic youth congresses which mushroomed in the 1980s, and technocrats returned from exile. The case of Mpumalanga is illustrative. Mpumalanga's MEC (or minister) for safety and security (until his resignation in 1997 in a car licensing scandal) was the former police minister of KwaNdebele homeland, Steve Skosana. Such people, when moving into the

ANC, often brought with them intact their patronage networks as well as grandiose expectations of privilege and deference. The habit shown by Inkatha MECs in KwaZulu-Natal of summoning detachments of civil servants to greet them at Ulundi airport is indicative of this. Nor are these reflexes confined to former homeland notables. The remark made by Mpumalanga's dismissed transport MEC, ex-Youth Leaguer Jackson Mthembu, when questioned about his decision to spend R2.3 million on a fleet of BMW 528s for his colleagues, was revealing: 'I am a leader in my community and therefore have a certain status – you can't be saying I should drive a 1600 cc vehicle.'[24]

Regional politics has also been dogged by intra-regional rivalries. In the Northern Province competition between politicians from the former homelands of Lebowa and Venda has promoted rival ethnic favouritism in different government departments. Premier Ngoako Ramatlhodi's administration was heavily weighted in favour of Northern Sotho politicians, partly a consequence of the recruitment of much of its leadership from the University of the North (the institution, incidentally, which has become the main *alma mater* of today's ascendant generation of national politicians). Ramatlhodi himself, who was Oliver Tambo's former private secretary, is viewed resentfully as an outsider imposed upon the local political establishment. In 1996 the regional Youth League nominated Peter Mokaba for the position of provincial chairman. Mokaba was persuaded by his cabinet colleagues in Cape Town to withdraw but conference delegates showed their displeasure by electing Senator George Mashamba instead. Ramatlhodi regained the leadership position in 1998 after a narrow victory over two of his MECs. In the meantime, he had attempted to create a degree of consensus in an increasingly unruly cabinet by firing five of his MECs to make room for leaders from the ANC's structures in the former Venda and Gazankulu homelands. Ethnic tensions seemed to have multiplied in the lower reaches of Ramatlhodi's administration: the suspension of the director-general of education was followed by rumours of a purge of Venda- and Shangaan-speaking civil servants. Before the ANC's 1997 conference, Ramatlhodi published a paper which argued in favour of the ANC ending its practice of making political appointments to top civil service positions. In the Northern Province some of the most politically insubordinate civil servants are recent political appointees.

Meanwhile, events in the Free State offered further evidence of leaders at odds with each other. On 20 June 1996, Premier Patrick 'Terror' Lekota dismissed from his 'cabinet' the economic affairs MEC, Ace Magashule, citing as his reason Magashule's 'insubordination'. This action provoked an immediate outcry within ANC provincial leadership circles. Lekota's critics claimed that he did not consult the party leadership adequately before dismissing Magashule. Lekota claims he did indeed consult both the cabinet and the ANC caucus in general terms several days before his reshuffle announcement. The chairman of the ANC executive in the province, Patrick Matosa made repeated calls for Lekota's resignation. Other members of the provincial leadership threatened a vote of no confidence in Lekota but were persuaded against this course by Cyril Ramaphosa. Over the subsequent weekend a delegation from the national government led by the minister of sport, Steve Tshwete, patched up a compromise in which Magashule was reinstated in the cabinet by being given the transport portfolio (recently surrendered by the National Party). As part of the agreement an advisory committee was to be established drawn from senior ANC leadership to facilitate consultations between the premier and the ANC.

Tensions continued to simmer. A meeting between Lekota and his critics on 26 July failed to resolve matters. Its main outcome was Lekota's loss of a seat on the provincial working committee. On 2 August, the National Working Committee of the ANC declined to debate 'the issue of confidence or no confidence' in Lekota. After listening to a report from Joe Nhlanhla (the deputy minister for intelligence services), Steve Tshwete and Arnold Stofile (the ANC's treasurer-general) on efforts to resolve problems in the province, the Committee decided that 'the status quo' should remain, and Lekota should keep the premiership. Meanwhile the Free State executive issued a statement criticising officials who had conspired to remove 'Comrade Lekota' from office, and who were using 'the organisation for personal and selfish reasons'. However, reports of conflict between Lekota and his executive persisted. Lekota was strengthened by a public declaration of support from the regional chairman, Stuurman Mokoena, on 6 September. That week civil servants marched on the ANC's Bloemfontein offices to ask it to end its 'harassment' of the premier.

There was a history of conflict between Lekota and his party executive. Ace Magashule is considered to be one of Lekota's primary political opponents and he was also vice-chairman of the provincial ANC. In 1993 the provincial party nominated Magashule for premier and he had to be asked to step down to make room for Lekota. At the 1994 ANC conference, Matosa and Magashule mounted a surprise challenge to Lekota in the leadership elections: Lekota, who had undertaken no lobbying before the meeting, came third in the delegates' poll.

Conflict between Lekota and Free State ANC leaders reflected local dissatisfaction at having a relative outsider imposed upon them by national leadership in 1994. Though Lekota was born in the province, in Kroonstad, he completed his secondary education in the Transkei, matriculated in Natal and spent his career as a political activist in Natal and the Transvaal. He spent six months in 1991 working as an ANC organiser in the northern Free State before being redeployed at head office, only returning to the Free State during the 1994 election campaign. Commentaries after the 1994 conference suggested that the main ground for the rift between Lekota and Matosa–Magashule was the belief that Lekota 'had taken reconciliation [with conservative whites] too far'. In April 1995 Lekota angered his critics further by suspending his housing MEC, Vax Mayekiso, for supposed involvement in an unsavoury property deal. Matosa said that Lekota had 'acted too fast'. Thereafter, Lekota suspended several senior officials suspected of dishonest dealings, and subsequently ANC legislators complained that these violated procedure.

On the surface, then, there appeared to be two issues separating Lekota from his colleagues: first, the resentment of local notables at having a relative outsider imposed in a leadership position over them, and secondly, a clash between the culture of accountability and consultation as understood among many activists who matured in the 1980s and Lekota's more imperious leadership style. In Matosa's words, in the ANC there was 'a tried and tested tradition . . . to collectively consult, but the premier seems to forget that he is accountable to the ANC as a political party'.[25] There may have been more to these tensions, though. Lekota enjoyed some support in the regional party leadership, and alignments in the cabinet suggest that a north–south rivalry helped to animate the quarrel. In an earlier dispute over the location of the provincial capital a strongly committed pro-Welkom faction emerged, headed by Mayekiso, Magashule and Matosa, each of them politicians whose support base was located in the northern Free State goldfields. This group also tended to favour 'socialist' rhetoric as opposed to the 'pragmatic' vein which Lekota prefers. The 'northerners' perceived their home area as underdeveloped in comparison to Bloemfontein and its environs, and they argued that Lekota's administration had been too sympathetically predisposed to white and emerging black elites in the capital. Kaizer Sebothelo, the party secretary, was also part of this group. It is true that since the 1994 election Lekota had developed good relationships with members of the old regime, in particular with Dr L. van der Watt, former Free State administrator, whom he appointed to his cabinet over the heads of the National Party hierarchy. Freedom Front leaders were also well disposed to Lekota. During the crisis Lekota also received public expressions of support from the editor of *Die Volksblad* and the chairman of the Free State Agricultural Union.

Ace Magashule's antipathy to Lekota may have had little to do with ideological or policy considerations. In August 1996 it was reported that he might be facing charges of misappropriating R7.88 million and authorising the payment of cheques into tourist promotion companies under his control. The ANC's initial reluctance to support Lekota in his dismissal of Magashule from his first portfolio arose apparently from the fact that Lekota referred the matter in June to the attorney-general without consulting the national leadership. Lekota may have been correct in terms of official procedure and law, but in choosing this route he offended traditional ANC protocol. As one of his political critics observed, 'Terror has confused the Constitution with convention.'[26] In December 1996, the auditor-general confirmed the validity of the allegations against Magashule. Five officials in the economic affairs and tourism department were suspended, three of whom belonged to the same branch as Magashule.

Lekota's supporters in the ANC leadership included Papi Kganare (the MEC for security), born in Thaba Nchu and with a background in trade unionism and the South African Youth Congress, mainly in Mangaung (Bloemfontein) and Vereeniging; Sakhiwo Belot (the MEC for education), a former teacher and an ANC branch secretary in Bloemfontein; Senorita Ntlabathi (the MEC for health), formerly a senior community nurse employed by the Bloemfontein city council; and Cas de Villiers (the MEC for agriculture). In the past, the ANC had been dominated by northerners because the north was where the organisation was most strongly developed, securing its foundations in the trade unions and community organisations established in the industrial towns near the Transvaal border in the 1980s. COSATU and SANCO both announced their support for Lekota, reflecting possibly the growth of unionism in the public sector and the spread of civics to Bloemfontein. However, Free State political organisation in 1996 was still volatile and fluid. Since 1994, the ANC had been developing its organisation where before it had none, in the huge squatter communities that were once part of the homelands of Bophuthatswana and QwaQwa where previously the ANC had found it either impossible or very difficult to function openly. QwaQwa activists tended to ally themselves with the Magashule group, for in the former homeland there was strong resentment among civil servants of Bloemfontein's centralisation of administration. In November, there were reports that Magashule partisans had undertaken the bulk distribution of free ANC membership cards in QwaQwa. In his previous capacity as chairman of the ANC's northern Free State region, Magashule enjoyed a reputation as an excellent organiser, even winning a prize from the ANC's headquarters for his efforts.

Meanwhile, the premier began attacking his rivals on a radio talk show, focusing on Magashule's financial dealings and Matosa's implication in a court case in which the ANC's provincial chairman was charged with attempted murder for drawing a gun on a traffic policeman. Until then, Lekota had never criticised his opponents in public, though his supporters had felt no such inhibitions: during August crowds attending political rallies would be worked into a frenzy with shouts of 'One Free State, One Lekota! Phantsi [Away with you], iOpportunisti, Phantsi!'

Lekota's radio commentaries prompted the ANC's National Executive to intervene once again. On 4 November Lekota and his cabinet were asked to resign and a caretaker committee for the province was appointed under the leadership of Tito Mboweni, then minister of labour. Despite protests by the Bloemfontein Taxi Forum which blockaded the legislature, a court case against the ANC for ignoring its own constitution, and continuing signals of dissent from the regional leaders of the ANC's trade union and communist allies, Mboweni's team proceeded with the selection and appointment of a new premier, another relative outsider, Ivy Matsepe-Casaburri, former head of the South African Broadcasting Corporation (SABC) board, and, like Lekota, a child of Kroonstad, but with a track record of mainly exile politics. In February 1997 the provincial ANC held a sullen conference. Casaburri's candidacy for the chairmanship was defeated by Zingile Dingane, chairman of the legislature's portfolio finance committee and a strong Lekota supporter. At this point Dingane was 'redeployed' to parliament in Cape Town along with Magashule and Lekota.

Casaburri's appointment did not end the ANC's troubles in this province. Contention between Magashule and Lekota loyalists continued through 1997 and 1998. In August 1998, provincial conference elections reversed the previous year's result. As a result of burgeoning branch organisation in Sasolburg, the Free State goldfields and QwaQwa as well as the reconstruction of the almost defunct Women's League by his supporters, Magashule won the chairmanship contest and an executive was elected composed of Lekota's former opponents, including Vax Mayekiso. Ivy Matsepe-Casaburri failed even to secure a nomination. Her efforts during the previous eighteen months to distance herself from the rival factions won her few friends. In the words of one of the delegates, 'she is seen as a person who is neutral. In politics there is no neutrality, a leader has to be firm and decisive. She did not want to be associated with any group.' Zingile Dingane's efforts to reconcile both groups engendered similar reactions: he was not nominated 'because he failed to pursue a certain agenda'.[27]

In Gauteng, political tensions of a different order surfaced in September 1997 with the election by representatives of 400 branches of a new premier, Mathole Motshekga, to replace Tokyo Sexwale, in defiance of the preferences of the incumbent party leadership and the provincial cabinet. Motshekga, chairman of the legislature's standing committee on development planning and local government, had chosen to decline a cabinet position in 1994 despite his senior party rank in the ANC. Although deputy chairman of the provincial organisation, he opted instead to devote his energies to consolidating a personal political following within the organisation. This he was able to achieve by building up a network of friendships with local councillors. His victory at the ANC's provincial council elections owed much to support from local councillors, especially those from outside Johannesburg, who felt, rightly or wrongly, that Soweto had received the lion's share of development resources in the province. His popularity was buttressed by his reputation as an 'Africanist', which was in turn bolstered by his status as a traditional healer and his exhortations for the revival of people's courts. He was helped also by the support of Mondli Gungubele, a former nurse and chair of the portfolio committee on public health, and as such a sharp critic of the executive's favoured candidate, the taciturn MEC for health, Amos Masondo. In July 1998, Gungubele replaced Masondo as health MEC. Masondo meanwhile underwent a rather surprising 'redeployment' to the ANC's headquarters to manage its 1999 election campaign. In a provincial executive drawn from a mixture of Johannesburg civic activists, communists, ex-trade unionists and technocrats, Motshekga's populism and his intellectual independence were deeply distrusted, a distrust which was manifested by a series of leakages to the press of allegations of corruption against him. In April 1998 an internal ANC commission of inquiry reported on these allegations against Motshekga. It cleared him of corruption charges but found that the premier had been a 'shambolic' manager at the National Institute for Public Interest Law which he had headed in the 1980s. The ANC should second appropriate people to help Motshekga run his government office more effectively, the commission advised. Since then, a succession of rhetorical indiscretions by the premier have continued to embarrass his colleagues while at the same time reports of continued factionalism directed at the premier have persisted.[28]

In addition to its recommendations respecting Motshekga, the commission also advocated a series of measures to halt 'creeping provincialism' within the ANC's ranks. In particular it suggested that provincial premiers should be appointed by the ANC president. This recommendation was endorsed by the ANC's executive in August 1998. In future premiers will be appointed by 'national structures' and the ANC provincial chairman will no longer automatically fill the post. The two positions will be 'delinked'. Premiers will be appointed in the same fashion as cabinet ministers. Such a measure supplies for the ANC leadership a constitutional method of preventing the ascendancy to executive positions of awkward personalities such as Mathole Motshekga. But it is unlikely to resolve the deeper causes of conflict in both Gauteng and the Free State, the fear within desperately poor communities that proximity to or distance from political leadership is the crucial determinant in influencing the allocation of public resources. In a political culture historically shaped by patron–client relations, politicians who fail to develop local bases and personal networks may simply end up pleasing nobody. The Free State history is a reminder about the complexity of internal ANC political relationships. Often tensions within the organisation are explained through references to the competitive solidarities produced by prison, exile or involvement in mass organisation during the 1980s. As the conflict between Magashule and Lekota, both former UDF leaders, demonstrated, the networks animated in ANC factionalism cannot be categorised so neatly.

What about popular perceptions of regional government? Survey evidence does not suggest in itself that provincial government has made the government generally more legitimate in the eyes of the citizenry. A report by the Institute for Democracy in South Africa (IDASA) on a survey conducted in late 1995 found significantly lower levels of public trust in provincial governments than in national government. A larger share of respondents (47 per cent) disapproved of their provincial rulers than approved (42 per cent); 53 per cent of the respondents, though, were pleased with the conduct of the national parliament. Mpumalanga, incidentally, received the highest trust rating (57 per cent), and the Northern Cape and the North West the best approval ratings.[29] Those provinces considered by specialists to be relatively well governed, namely Gauteng and the Western Cape, received relatively bad ratings. This may be a consequence of the social diversity and political divisions within their populations as well as relatively higher political expectations.

However, these survey revelations need not be taken to imply that provincial governments necessarily *detract* from overall government legitimacy. Indeed they may supply a focus for public dissatisfaction which might otherwise be directed at national government. Some of the shortcomings I have described may help to improve public opinion. For example, the existence of a well-organised patronage system which distributes political goods quite widely may make government seem accessible and responsive at least to those citizens who benefit. The border dispute which erupted in Bushbuckridge in 1997 was significant in this respect. Here, people who had been oriented politically to the networks centred around Nelspruit, in the new province of Mpumalanga, found themselves incorporated into the Northern Province, governed by a distant bureaucracy in Pietersburg with weak social links to the district. Local people felt they would get better treatment from Nelspruit officials, who in any case could be reached by only a two-hour taxi ride as opposed to an overnight journey to Pietersburg. What the border conflict also demonstrated was the way in which popular political affiliations are in the process of being reconstructed around regionalism. In a research project on social movements in which I have been collaborating since 1994, there has emerged an evident geographical redistribution of activist politics, away from their traditional concentration in the big towns and towards the new regional centres. This augurs well for democracy, we believe.[30]

The ANC's national leadership is, reportedly, increasingly concerned about the costs, both financial and political, of regionalism. At its 1997 Mafikeng conference, Nelson Mandela's speech referred to the need for a new theoretical thinking about the shape of the post-apartheid state. ANC constitutional experts are believed to favour the reduction of the provincial governments to mere administrations, removing from them their representative and elected components and subordinating their civil services to the national departments. They can only do this, though, if the ANC wins 66 per cent of the vote in the 1999 election, or if they secure another party's agreement to such a move, both unlikely developments. More plausible is the possibility of reducing the scope of provincial power by enlarging the authority of local governments through the construction of unified 'megacities' with much greater administrative capacity than today's municipalities.

I think both courses would be mistaken. The administrative failings of regional bureaucracies will not disappear if they lose their constitutional status, and the task of supervising them from Pretoria will become no easier. Megacities will only relocate the political problems, as well as the patronage networks, lower down the state hierarchy, as is happening already with housing, a field in which local authorities are beginning to assume responsibility from regional government without discernibly better results. In any case, the proceedings I have been describing may not signify breakdown, but rather may represent the conflicts and struggles which are the inevitable effect of change, a process of which the outcome is still uncertain. To help us in our predictions as to how beneficial change will be, we need to look more closely at the government's efforts to reallocate resources to create a better life, and evaluate such efforts more carefully. We turn to these tasks in the next chapter.

3

THE RDP:
DELIVERY AND PERFORMANCE

The essentials of the Reconstruction and Development Programme (RDP) can be captured in a couple of paragraphs. The
Programme emphasised two aims: the alleviation of poverty, and
the reconstruction of the economy. These two objectives were
interrelated, the RDP's authors maintained. Balanced economic
growth was impossible without the simultaneous promotion of
economic development. Without growth there could be no
development. Economic growth without development would fail
to bring about 'structural transformation', that is, a more
advanced economy and a more equitable and prosperous society.
Policies concentrated purely on promoting growth would accen-
tuate existing inequalities and maintain mass poverty, and these
would soon stifle growth. The government, the RDP insisted,
should play 'a major enabling role' in integrating growth with
economic reconstruction and social development.

The RDP proposed five ways to combine growth with development: (1) meeting basic needs, (2) upgrading human resources,
(3) strengthening the economy, (4) democratising the state and
society, and (5) reorganising the state and the public sector. These
activities should involve and empower ordinary people: 'development is not just about the delivery of goods to a passive citizenry'. The RDP should be 'people-driven', that is, it should deepen
democracy by enabling people affected by development projects
to participate in their planning. Economic reconstruction and
social development should be mutually reinforcing. Expansion of
infrastructure would stimulate and strengthen the economy and

provide popular access to better services. A more modern infrastructure, the RDP suggested, would help to improve South African export capacity.

Such improvements were badly needed, the RDP insisted, for the South African economy was afflicted with a 'deep structural crisis'. Manufacturing was unproductive and dependent on low wages and imported machinery. It made a meagre contribution to foreign exchange earnings and it failed to create new jobs. Within the wider industrial economy, heavily concentrated ownership 'create[d] social tension' and prevented competition. Labour worked inefficiently and its historic repression retarded the accumulation of skills. Heavily subsidised commercial agriculture was often inefficient. Government expenditure required high personal taxation and a growing deficit. Meanwhile private capital flowed out of the country.

'Neither commandist central planning nor unfettered free markets' could remedy these problems. The public sector would be needed to 'strengthen the ability of the economy to respond to inequalities' and to promote growth. It might even have to be enlarged, the RDP speculated, 'through, for example, nationalization'. On the other hand, it might have to be reduced. Privatisation measures might promote efficiency, affirmative action, and in general 'empower the historically oppressed'. Government, trade unions, business and civil society organisations should co-operate in redirecting the economy. Labour policies should stress education, training, 'a living wage' and collective bargaining. Affirmative action should include 'massive' training programmes, anti-discriminatory measures in hiring and promotion, job security for pregnant women, and the development of local expertise in preference to the 'import of outsiders'. The public sector would set an example: within two years, 'recruitment and training should reflect South African society in terms of race and gender'.

Economic restructuring should be geared to increasing national investment in manufacturing, job creation and basic needs. South Africa should become a significant exporter of manufactures. Internationally competitive industries should be strengthened and integrated better with other sectors of economic activity. Anti-trust legislation would be needed to spread and de-racialise business ownership. Foreign investors should receive the same treatment as South African businessmen. Policies should ensure that foreign investment 'creates as much employment and real knowledge transfer as possible'. The government should help small and especially black-owned enterprises through its allocation of contracts and by requiring financial banks to lend more capital to small firms. In agriculture, subsidies and controls should be removed and support services given to those in greatest need – 'poor farmers, especially women'. The expensive pursuit of self-sufficiency in food should be abandoned and farming encouraged to become more labour-intensive and environmentally sustainable.

The RDP also expected the private sector to contribute to fulfilling basic needs. Some of the basic needs proposals were clearly intended to be implemented mainly through government activities. These included the rationalisation of existing health expenditure and services in favour of primary health care; a public works programme to provide employment and supply clean water and electrical connections to communities without them; land reforms to redistribute 30 per cent of the land under commercial agriculture; and the institution of feeding schemes to ensure basic nutritional requirements. Private companies, though, were expected to collaborate with the government in constructing a million low-cost houses and helping the poorest people buy them.

Reconstruction and development should be an all-embracing effort, the programme's drafters exhorted. 'Development forums' would bring together 'all major stakeholders' in formulating and implementing RDP projects. These bodies should represent political parties, NGOs, business and community associations. Organisations in civil society 'must be encouraged to develop their own RDP programmes of action and campaigns within their own sectors'. The RDP should not increase government expenditure significantly, its planners warned. Many of its objectives could be accomplished through the reallocation of government expenditure. Market forces could also achieve certain RDP goals. For instance, deregulating agriculture would, the RDP's authors hoped, release resources for redistribution. Socially desirable investments by the private sector, for example in low-cost housing, would represent a major contribution to RDP financing. Much of the economic growth and restructuring would be prompted by the expansion of consumer demand, which would follow the building of houses and the extension of electricity and piped water. Better labour productivity would follow the institution of education and training programmes.[31]

The RDP has meant different things to different people. There was a 'left' understanding of the RDP which probably conformed with the way most political activists understood the programme. COSATU and SACP leaders tended to read the RDP as a 'decisive break' with past policies; in particular, they emphasised those sections in the document 'which demonstrate the economic value of particular types of state intervention in the economy'.[32] Their understanding of the RDP was encapsulated quite well at the SACP's 9th Congress in 1995. The RDP had four essential dimensions, delegates were reminded. These were: (1) redistribution – this should be a central characteristic of government activity; (2) economic reconstruction, along a new growth path directed at 'inward development'; (3) the state's assumption of the role of coordinator of development; and (4) development as a 'people-centred' or 'people-driven' process.

This was not the only way the RDP was understood, though. The government, in its 1994 RDP White Paper, which committed itself to restricting the growth of the public sector as well as endorsing privatisation,[33] seemed to interpret the RDP in a less populist fashion. The ambiguity in the original 'base document' provided plenty of authority for more socially conservative readings of the RDP. Much of the programme's language accorded well with current orthodoxies among development agencies concerning the role of the state, 'not as a direct provider of growth but as a partner, catalyst, and facilitator',[34] with private enterprise participating in the provision of welfare and utilities. Business supporters of the RDP,[35] taking their cue from such an aphorism, drew attention to a different set of the programme's features:

(1) development as a process which depends upon a partnership between the state and private enterprise; (2) a thinner, more efficient, less expensive state; (3) an internationally competitive economy; and (4) a better-educated and more productive workforce. There have been other more cynical views among businessmen. Especially notorious was the remark made in 1995 by the chairman of Barlow Rand, who gleefully told a shareholders' meeting that his company 'would be feeding off the carcass of the RDP for years to come'.[36]

Finally, there were the popular expectations about the RDP. Political parties which polled public sentiment before the 1994 election generally found a consistent ranking of the things that people felt a democratic government should achieve: jobs (above all else), water (in rural areas), houses, peace, land. Understandably, this was the way in which the ANC projected the RDP to its supporters, as a programme geared to meeting basic needs, during the 1994 general election.

Ordinary people were most inclined to understand the RDP as the provision of benefits and opportunities: a better living environment, improved services, and enhanced life chances. It is quite reasonable to begin an evaluation of the RDP by considering the government's achievements with respect to these popular expectations. To what extent has the government succeeded in creating 'a better life for all'?

The statistics are quite impressive. Here are some of the more significant figures:[37]

• With respect to primary health care. New clinics have treated 8.5 million patients since April 1994. In 1997 ten new or upgraded clinics became operational every week, more than 500 altogether. The beneficiaries of this activity include 52,000 people who have had their sight restored.[38] In 1995, a polio-hepatitis vaccination programme began and two years later it had immunised 8 million children.[39]

• Land reform. Some 68,000 families have been settled on 220,000 hectares of farming land. This is still a long way from the RDP goal of redistributing 30 per cent of commercial land within five years; 220,000 hectares is about 1.5 per cent of the commercial farmland. Within four years 250,000 people had 'received land', the authorities claimed.[40]

• Housing. Since 1994 about 600,000 cheap houses eligible for government subsidy either have been built or are under construction (about 250,000 are said to be completed).[41] A further 250,000 housing subsidies had been granted for projected housing schemes by May 1998.[42]

• Roads. Altogether 154 rural roads, totalling 1500 kilometres, were built by the Public Works Project between 1994 and 1997.

• Clean water. By the beginning of 1998, standpipes had been installed within 200 metres of the dwellings of about 1.3 million rural people who previously either used ground water or bought their drinking supplies from lorries. In 1997 alone, half a million people gained access to clean piped water in this way. In August 1998 the minister of water affairs, Kader Asmal, stated that since he took office 'more than 2.5 million people had been given access to fresh safe water for the first time'.[43]

• Electrification. Up to the end of 1997 and since 1994, 1.4 million homes were connected to the national grid, 420,000 alone in 1998. By 1998, 58 per cent of the South African population lived in dwellings with electricity. In mid-1996, according to the census, 4 million South African homes had electricity.

Numbers can be misleading, but these statistics really do signify considerable change. In the case of water, though, the million beneficiaries of the new standpipes need to be considered against the 12 million who were without access to piped water in 1994. Before then, most rural water provision was oriented to the needs of commercial agriculture, and by 1994, 75 per cent of the water installations which had been established in the homelands since 1980 had ceased to function.[44]

With respect to housing, during the apartheid era housing peaked in 1990 at 50,000 subsidised units built for Africans. The current rate of home-building exceeds the total erected in the period 1955–65, the previous era of really extensive mass housing construction.[45] Modern Soweto accommodates about 125,000 houses, a figure which suggests the quite impressive scope of the government's programme. About 2.6 million houses for the about 7 million people living today in shanty settlements are still needed, though.[46]

Land reform was virtually non-existent before 1994 in the sense in which it is being undertaken today. As late as 1984 government was still taking land purchased by their ancestors away from black farmers in the western Transvaal.[47]

The impact of primary health care is signalled by falling infant mortality statistics, from 51 per thousand in 1994[48] to 40.2 per thousand in 1996,[49] a consequence of free access to maternity care since 1994 and immunisation programmes. In 1996 an opinion poll indicated that 63 per cent of South Africans believed they had better access to health care than before.[50]

The greater proportion of these changes has resulted from re-allocations of government expenditure rather than through increasing national taxation or raising public borrowing. As the RDP's authors advocated, government expenditure has remained, in real terms, more or less at 1994 levels, while the Department of Finance succeeded in reducing the deficit progressively in 1996, 1997 and 1998. The costs of these programmes are evident, however, in a variety of ways. The removal of farmers' subsidies as well as labour reforms helps to explain the huge job losses in agriculture; in 1994 commercial farmers employed 1.4 million people whereas in 1998 this number had fallen to 637,000. Both agricultural unions and SANCO suggest that violent crime directed against farmers is often undertaken by the disaffected sons of former farmworkers.[51] Increasing the primary health care budget has required the diversion of funds from hospitals. Despite coping with accelerating numbers of patients, urban hospitals, including those serving poor communities, have had to contend with 30 per cent staff cuts,[52] and their services have deteriorated dramatically. Less consequential costs include higher school fees for more affluent suburban parents; rate hikes accompanied by the withdrawal of certain municipal services in wealthy neighbourhoods; and sharp reductions in defence expenditure.

Most fair-minded people would concede that certain sacrifices are reasonable if these reforms and improvements in government services directed at poor communities are sustained and have long-lasting effects. This is when making judgments about the RDP's effectiveness becomes more problematic: we need to consider the quality of services and resources now under delivery to citizens, not just the quantity.

Let us take water as a case study. Water provision is a high-profile programme, of which the government is very proud. The Department of Water Affairs is headed by a charismatic and popular politician, Kader Asmal, who has animated the public imagination with what he calls 'new South African ablutions'.[53] To its great credit, the Department has taken pains to make sure that its efforts are professionally evaluated. To this end, in 1997 it commissioned an NGO, the Mvula Trust, which had a specialised concern with the issues connected with supplying water to rural people, to undertake an investigation of some of the projects the Department had established.[54]

Mvula's researchers focused on three projects, at Winterveldt (in the North West), at Shemula (KwaZulu-Natal) and at Kgobokwane (Mpumalanga). These three projects served a total of nearly 300,000 people, about a quarter of those then affected by the Department's water provisions. From the investigations of Mvula's consultants it became clear that the most important determinant of the success of the projects was the degree of community engagement with their conception and management. At the outset, the Department acknowledged in principle the need for the projects to be planned in such a way that the beneficiaries would feel they owned them and hence recognised they were responsible for their upkeep. In practice this proved to be quite difficult. In only one of these projects, Kgobokwane (in Mpumalanga), did there exist a lively culture of democratically organised 'community based organisations' (CBOs). In this area there were branches of SANCO as well as a local network of the Rural Women's Movement: these bodies had elected a Water Committee in 1994, in anticipation of government action.

In Shemula there also existed a community-based movement, the Amazi Development Trust. In Winterveldt no such organisation existed, partly because of social tensions which had their origin in conflicts between tenants and freehold landlords in the area. In the case of Kgobokwane and Winterveldt, the planning and management of the projects was entrusted to the local authority. This was a difficult decision to justify with respect to Kgobokwane and owed much to the personal predispositions of the officials concerned. In Shemula, the Development Trust was accorded the task of managing the project. Rural local councils are not always very effective institutions. They are often responsible for huge and scattered areas and they only have advisory functions.

In examining the way each of these projects operated, the Mvula consultants found the extent of community involvement to be the key factor in all sorts of ways: in the initial design of the project, in assessing demand and people's willingness to pay for water, in preventing illegal tapping of the water supply, and in maintaining the scheme and collecting the income from it. None of the projects was covering its running costs at the time of the fieldwork, partly because of inaccurate projections of demand but also because only in the case of Shemula were people actually paying for the water they consumed. When people did pay for their water they appeared not to be consuming more than they used to buy from the tank carriers. Thus even when the schemes are working they may not make such a difference to people's lives except in shortening the distance over which water needs to be carried. In certain schemes, payment levels have been affected by the operation of other, externally financed schemes, installed by the old homeland governments. As one Mvula manager has observed, 'communities with new systems, perhaps rightly, began questioning why they were paying for services when neighbouring villages received free water'.[55]

It is a mixed picture, then. The Department's commitment to monitoring its own achievements is impressive. The shortcomings are attributable mainly to haste, authoritarian inclinations among officials in the field, and inadequate research and planning. But unless these tendencies are corrected the water schemes may be short-lived. At the workshop at which this report was presented it was pointed out that of the new schemes about a quarter had ceased to function because of neglect and damage to the installations.

In a short book, there is not the space to survey all the RDP initiatives, but housing deserves some consideration because it is so politically conspicuous. Here there are two types of problems. The first concerns costs and pricing. The way the housing strategy works is by the government awarding subsidies to prospective homeowners through a complex process in which private sector developers propose schemes that qualify for these subsidies. The state does not actually build the houses. Initially, the delays in housing construction were the result of bureaucratic bottlenecks – it took a long time for the authorities to approve schemes. The process has been decentralised so that powers of approval are invested in municipalities. This has accelerated the pace of housing construction but at the expense of efficient control.

This raises the second issue, that of quality. A subsidy of R15,000 does not go very far towards covering the cost of even a very basic dwelling, not once the land has been serviced with plumbing, sewers and access roads. Official policy favours the participation of small local contractors and self-help schemes – there are several cases of *stokvels* (small credit schemes) undertaking the task of housing construction – though the initial bids are often made by large companies, which then sub-contract. Small contractors usually build more expensive houses because they cannot employ economies of scale or sophisticated construction systems.[56] Some of the cheapest houses have been built by women's self-help groups, based on *stokvel* schemes. In Soweto such a group in Protea helped by an NGO, the South African Homeless People's Federation, builds houses for its members for R10,000 each, financing the houses and building them through rotating allocations of cash and collective labour, making their own bricks and using second-hand materials. The Protea scheme started without housing subsidies and the dwellings they constructed would cost R50,000 through a normal RDP venture in Soweto employing contractors.[57] Official policy notwithstanding, self-help groups often complain of disdainful treatment by subsidy administrators.[58]

Bureaucratic regulations may work against self-help groups but they do not always effectively restrain commercial operators.

There is no general standardised set of regulations concerning design, planning or pricing. In several notorious cases the profit margins awarded to themselves by private contractors have been very high. Motheo Construction, the firm awarded a contract to build 10,000 houses in Mpumalanga and headed by a friend of the housing minister, is one example of this trend. In East Rand's Phola Park, HBM, a company directed by Winnie Madikizela-Mandela, attempted to win a contract from the Presidential Project management committee, by skirting regulations and assembling a showhouse, twice the size and three times the cost of other developers' models.[59] Another example of a firm which probably benefits from its political connections is LVR Construction, a company building houses in the Free State and owned by a local political notable and former provincial chairman of the legislature's housing committee, Ace Magashule. Nor has there been a systematic strategy of assessing where housing is most needed, and where shortages are most likely to occur in the future.

Many of the completed estates are poorly planned, though certainly an improvement on squatter encampments. There are too many straight rows of boxy dwellings lacking social amenities and situated far away from the places where their residents work, constructed as they are on the cheapest land available. Are they always better than what they replace? I travelled recently through what used to be Venda, and by the road you could see neat thatched villages of mud-walled houses and compounds laid out in the way people obviously prefer them. Next to these sociable settlements there were chequerboard grids of new zinc-roofed brick huts with no shade or convivial spaces. In Soweto, a Johannesburg architect noted in 1996 that the new housing schemes he visited barely differed, in overall planning, layout, type of construction and quality of finish, from 'the massive building programmes that occurred during the 1950s and 1960s'. Both consisted of crabbed interiors, regimented streets, dormitory tracts, estates not neighbourhoods.[60] It is difficult to see such bleak developments as 'empowering' or 'people-driven', however much income they may have generated for local builders.

How successful has the government been in realising its objectives in the Reconstruction and Development Programme? This depends upon whose criteria of success serve as the basis for evaluation. If we keep in mind the 'left' version of the RDP, with its emphases on redistribution, inward economic reconstruction, state coordination of development and popular participation, the record is uneven. With respect to redistribution, within the limits of conservative public finance there has taken place a fairly substantial reallocation of resources and services. The relatively low cost of this and its impact in certain quarters do represent a real indictment of the old regime. So much more could have been achieved when goods and services were cheaper than they are today.

The scorecard for economic progress is less substantial. Except in the vaguest terms, government has yet to publish an industrial policy that will identify the priorities for public investment so as to encourage certain kinds of economic venture. The left's argument that growth will be significantly boosted by the new domestic markets for manufactures created by better living standards represents a prospect which is still fairly remote, though electrification could play a very important part in expanding local markets.

The state's capacity as a coordinator has been quite weak. Development projects, with notable exceptions like water, are implemented through provincial governments, and, as we have seen, both their political complexity and their bureaucratic shortcomings make implementation of development policies extraordinarily difficult. Coordination requires imagination and vision, and the state's managers have often chosen to ignore the NGO sector, which frequently possesses the appropriate experience and knowledge of what is needed. It is also worrying that state policies themselves are often poorly integrated to achieve the most important goals. For example, regulations which compel the use of generic medicines may cheapen the cost of public health but this is at the cost of foreign investment by drug companies in a potentially very competitive export-oriented local industry.

Finally, the state's commitment to people-driven development seems to have been fluctuating and ambivalent. In many areas the trend has run against popular participation; the current emphasis in housing policy, for example, is on 'mass provision'. The collapse of the development forums and the weakness of community-based organisations make it all the more difficult to engage citizens in development projects.

What about the business community's expectations of the RDP? Certainly there is plenty of evidence of the state's willingness to share the responsibility for meeting 'basic needs' with private enterprise, sometimes, its critics argue, to the detriment of the supposed beneficiaries of such programmes. It may be significant, for example, that some of the most imaginatively designed housing schemes have been inner-city terraced housing, which will remain within the public sector to accommodate rent-paying tenants.[61] Business would like to see a smaller and less expensive state; given the political pressures for job provision the government has demonstrated restraint in not enlarging the public payroll. South African economic competitiveness remains restricted by low levels of worker productivity and, corporate spokesmen argue, legislation that promotes labour market inflexibility. Better-educated and hence more productive workers seem a remote prospect given the government's failure to improve the quality of public schooling.[62]

Politicians, though, are not businessmen; they cannot be expected to arrange their priorities using the same values as stockbrokers. Government programmes have attempted to address a range of concerns across a deeply divided society. The shortcomings of public policy in its conception and implementation have reflected these divisions but the limited achievements are all the more impressive because of them.

4

LOCAL ELECTIONS AND
MUNICIPAL POLITICS

Probably the most difficult tasks in the creation of a socially integrated democracy in South Africa are those which must be
undertaken by local government, for it is over the local allocation
of resources that the material conflicts between South Africa's different communities are most evident. White South Africans tend
to measure government performance by the quality of services
administered in their neighbourhoods: street cleaning, well-main-
tained public spaces, efficient electricity supplies, regular public
transport, smoothly tarred roads, and so forth – all the normal
responsibilities of local authorities. Many of the public goods
which black South Africans expect as the consequence of their
enfranchisement – clinics, street lighting, water-borne sewerage –
are also delivered by municipal administrations.

The local government arrangements that were institutionalised
in the 1993 Constitution reflected a rather different understanding of democracy than the vision of community empowerment
and participatory democracy which black civic associations and
street committees attempted to promote in the townships in the
1980s. In particular the scale of many local authorities as well as
the incorporation of list-style proportional representation would
weaken accountability in the new institutions. This was partly
compensated for by the retention of (very large) wards for 60 per
cent of the representation in town councils. But the equal split
between wards in former statutory (white or coloured or Indian)
neighbourhoods and those in black townships, regardless of the
size of their populations, meant that in most places blacks would

be under-represented.[63]

Nationally, in November 1995 only 5.3 million people voted for nearly 700 councils, about a quarter of the number that participated in the general election one year previously, and about 45 per cent of those who were entitled to do so.[64] In the most urbanised province, Gauteng, only 39 per cent of potential voters participated.[65] This was a bit disappointing if one views these elections as a key moment in the birth of authentic local democracy.[66] The results suggested other, less obvious insights, however, which may have been more encouraging for democrats generally, not just those affiliated to the ANC. In the general election of 1994 black voting was practically uniformly favourable to the ANC (except in KwaZulu-Natal) and many commentators complained that the general elections were in effect a 'racial census'.[67] In the local elections of 1995 it was still true that in most black wards the ANC received more than 90 per cent of the vote (and 66 per cent of the overall total) but this was not always the case and the exceptions were interesting.

In Midrand–Ivory Park, a 'non-political' ratepayers' Community Action Party (CAP) contested wards in both squatter camps and patrician suburban estates and did surprisingly well in each. Altogether CAP obtained 9016 ward votes to the ANC's 13,416, running a strong second to the ANC amongst the Ivory Park squatters. CAP candidates were an eclectic mixture: some had previous National Party (NP) associations, one belonged to the ANC and another had once presided over a Pan Africanist Congress (PAC) branch. Several had longstanding involvements in residents' associations, both black and white. Black independents did well in several other Gauteng communities, in Sebokeng near Vereeniging and on the East Rand, for example. A common feature in their success seems to have been locally weak and fractious ANC organisations, and their own prominence within local civic associations or SANCO branches. SANCO–ANC tensions were a conspicuous feature of the campaign after several SANCO nominees were highhandedly removed from ANC lists in February 1995.[68] Thus, confronted with plausible candidates, black voters made discriminating choices.

For most township residents, though, the historically white parties seemed to have no credibility even when they put up strong local candidates. This was the case in Alexandra, near Sandton, with the Democratic Party (DP) whose star performer, Walter Mojapelo, a former ANC notable and a well-known community leader who had run feeding and educational schemes, obtained a dispiriting 74 votes. The DP only did well in one Alexandra ward, number 22, in the vicinity of an up-market housing project. Here Linda Rammutla collected 510 votes, not enough to win but sufficient to be taken seriously. Outside middle-class township enclaves at this stage, only parties which had a constant community presence had prospects of enlisting black support. In effect this meant the ANC and Inkatha Freedom Party (IFP); in most townships the PAC had minimal organisation and in November 1995 its black candidates were often unknown locally.

Another pointer to a less communally monolithic politics in the future is the extent to which in certain locations outside black townships people voted across historic racial and party divisions. In Johannesburg the ANC assembled a list of well-known white candidates and some of these did sufficiently well to suggest that their following was genuinely non-racial. Their share of the vote was well in excess of black voter registration in suburban neighbourhoods. This was a particular feature of the Eastern Metropolitan Substructure (EMSS) of Johannesburg, an area in which the DP also did well. What is likely is that traditionally liberal white voters were increasingly predisposed to vote ANC as well as DP. This trend was also evident in the later election for the Cape Town Metropolitan Council in which the ANC claimed to have obtained the support of 15 per cent of white voters, 'a support base we never had'.[69] In Midrand the ANC won the mainly white Ward One with an Indian candidate who devoted a major part of her campaigning to house visits among her affluent white neighbours.

In Roshnee, outside Vereeniging, the PAC candidate did well, gaining 815 votes to nearly match his ANC rival. He had the advantage of being Indian in an Indian ward, whereas the ANC candidate was coloured. But it was a significant result for the

PAC, a party with a history of only occasional support within the Indian community. The PAC's Roshnee candidate, Amin Lutchka, was a well-known local doctor, former ANC member, and active person in various Islamic welfare organisations. His manifesto emphasised conservative themes: flat rates, educational standards, and opposition to gay rights, abortion and pornography. In Gauteng, the ANC generally did well among Indian communities but coloured voters divided about evenly, right and left, as they did in the general election. Around Johannesburg the NP assembled a strong list of candidates, some with good civic association records. In the end, though, they had to rest content with winning one black ward, Newclare, but they would have won seats in other coloured neighbourhoods had they not shared the anti-ANC vote with a right-wing civic movement, the South-Western Johannesburg Civic Association (SOWEJOCA). Ironically, defensive ethnic consciousness could itself prompt 'cross-over' politics. This was evident in Johannesburg's southern suburbs where SOWEJOCA and the IFP made a point of targeting poor whites. The IFP's Themba Khoza went so far as to organise a monthly food parcel distribution for pensioners in the poor suburb of Moffatview.

These features of the election do not represent seismic shifts but they may indicate the slow consolidation of a post-nationalist political culture. There were signals that such a culture may become more tolerant of diversity. Most of the DP's complaints about intimidation were limited to the removal and destruction of its posters though several of its candidates did receive death threats. An ugly reminder of the murderous atmosphere which had prevailed in certain districts two years earlier was the ambush and shooting of six IFP candidates in Lochiel, in Mpumalanga.[70] The November 1995 polls omitted two of the main areas of previous electoral thuggery, KwaZulu-Natal and Cape Town, though the contests in these regions the following year were comparatively sedate. Police spokesmen, apparently, did think there was generally less misbehaviour in their districts. A national survey conducted by the Human Sciences Research Council (HSRC)[71] in August asked people to respond to the assertion that 'only those political parties that are popular in my community should be allowed to campaign'. Amongst black members of the sample surveyed, 40 per cent were in agreement and another 16 per cent were uncertain: depressingly similar proportions to comparable questions asked in opinion polls before the general elections. Nearly 30 per cent of whites also agreed with this view. Not surprisingly, this kind of intolerance seemed to correlate with youth, poverty and educational deprivation. The ostensibly better conduct in the local elections thus probably reflected merely lack of interest rather than changing attitudes – generally in black townships, only a minority of eligible voters participated.

What were the elections about? Were they merely a mid-term referendum on the government's performance or did they reflect genuine popular engagement with local politics? The main parties piously declared in advance that this was to be a contest about local communities 'empowering themselves', vowing that the campaign should be 'locally driven' with neighbourhood folk in the forefront. The ANC produced a national manifesto that emphasised local democracy, community involvement, public accountability, gender equity and non-racial unity. Its campaign manual instructed its local election teams 'to build on the core national message and make it more concrete' by relating its themes 'to the problems and concerns of the voters we are targeting'.[72] This happened in certain areas but, all too frequently, local ANC candidates failed to project specifically local concerns.

In Gauteng, the ANC produced a leaflet for each candidate, bearing his or her name and picture above the slogan 'A better life: Let's make it happen here'. In each case, though, the text on the obverse side was identical, stressing the ANC's commitment to fighting crime through community policing forums, ensuring public access to housing subsidies, expanding and maintaining services, and improving pension pay-out arrangements. Two of these, housing subsidies and pension payments, were of course administered by provincial government, not local authorities. ANC discomfort at having to address the crime issue, perceived at the time to be principally a 'white' preoccupation, was reflected in its slogan borrowed from the British Labour Party's 'Tough on crime: Tough on the causes of crime'. Its own effort 'Fight crime: Let's make it happen here' was more original but equally unpersuasive.

Too frequently, ANC meetings were built around 'big name' crowd-pullers. For example, an evening meeting in Coronationville in Johannesburg on 17 October mainly featured Tokyo Sexwale. The three local candidates were dispensed with in five minutes each, barely enough time for them to supply basic biographies, let alone to develop their proposals for communal governance, before the regional premier took the rostrum for over an hour. In much of this time Sexwale devoted his address to attacking Basil Douglas of SOWEJOCA, Tony Leon of the DP, and F.W. de Klerk of the NP, telling his audience about his new youth pilot training scheme, blaming white farmers for the squatter problem, and promising investment from Japan.

The DP and the NP drew up more municipally oriented programmes and many of their candidates did indeed produce detailed local manifestos, often drawing upon their own resources to do so. Even so, national leadership was highly conspicuous both in campaigning and on posters. Both parties chose to accent crime in their publicity. DP proposals included municipally controlled policing together with privatisation of other services, fair rates and sanctions against those who did not pay them. Centrally produced NP propaganda attacked the ANC for failing to deliver on RDP promises, complained about illegal immigrants into the country and called for more funding for the police. The IFP manifesto promised local crime commissions, the improvement of the business environment, and 'opposition to the government's forced modernisation' of rural areas. This last concern also featured in the PAC programme, which pledged to protect traditional leaders, generate self-help projects, discourage drug abuse and allocate 'more sites for religious purposes'. As can be seen, all the main parties fought the election around issues which were often tangential to the concerns of local government and, in Gauteng at least, none of them produced coherent programmes addressed to the particular concerns of specific towns. To be fair, however, ward candidates often attempted to compensate for this neglect by emphasising neighbourhood preoccupations.

How did the voters perceive the election? What for them were the most important issues? The HSRC survey offered respondents five national goals to which they had to assign priority: 70 per cent of whites chose 'maintaining order' as opposed to only 20 per cent of black respondents; for 56 per cent of the latter, creating more jobs was the main issue. Wits University fieldworkers[73] around Johannesburg discovered that in white areas, particularly poorer districts and outlying suburbs, the fear generated by squatter land occupations was the issue which arose most spontaneously; none of the main parties had systematic or coherent policies on squatting. The focus on crime, though, was politically well calculated: the fieldworkers found it to be a common preoccupation among candidates and their audiences across the social spectrum.

Community empowerment, one of the ANC's main themes, appeared from the survey not to be a major preoccupation. Of the black respondents 40 per cent agreed with the sentiment that 'popular participation is not necessary if decision-making is left in the hands of a few trusted competent leaders', 38 per cent disagreed and 21 per cent were uncertain. Whites were even less predisposed towards participatory politics: 57 per cent of the white sample agreed with the statement and only 33 per cent opposed it. For half of black respondents, now that a democratic system of local government existed 'we no longer have a need for organisations like civics and street committees', and less than a third felt otherwise. Roughly equal one-third minorities of blacks concurred and differed with the opinion that local government should have the power to adopt policies that conflict with those of other levels of government. All these responses suggest that the new authorities would enjoy considerable legitimacy despite the fact that most of the respondents failed to identify correctly the municipal administration they lived in.

In most cases, legitimacy was the new councils' primary asset. In 1995 virtually every major local government faced a financial crisis. There were two dimensions to this. Firstly there was a huge backlog of bad debts resulting from the continued failure of most householders in townships and squatter camps to pay rentals and service charges. In the town in which the rent boycott started, Vereeniging, the situation was fairly typical: here the municipal deficit increased by R3 million every month. In 1996, a successful council workers' strike pushed the annual salary bill from R60 to R87 million. The existence of popularly elected local authorities might have boosted hopes that the government's much punted 'Masakhane' programme to encourage payment for services would be more successful in the aftermath of the election. Its director, Chris Ngcobo, complained in September 1995 that 'councillors did not take the campaign seriously and most are too scared to tell people to pay for services because they want to save face for the elections'.[74] Whether, even if they were willing, simply 'telling' people would be enough, was questionable. At the same time sanctions of the kind advocated by the ANC's opponents would be extremely unpopular. The HSRC survey found 57 per cent of its black respondents opposed to evictions or cessation of services to those who failed to pay for them.

In any case, the problems would not have ended with the restoration of a full 'culture of payment'. Even if people met their obligations the financial base of local government would be inadequate and unsustainable. The newly unified municipalities would soon experience conflicts between rich and poor communities over the allocation of resources and the discrepancies between tariffs and rates charged in affluent neighbourhoods and those charged in impoverished ones. In 1995, before the elections, certain councils attempted to anticipate this conflict. Conservative Witbank, for example, in the run-up to the poll, increased electricity and water charges for black township residents. Whites were evidently strongly opposed to cross-subsidisation: in the HSRC survey only 37 per cent thought that 'taxes of the wealthy should be spent to upgrade poor communities'. In the metropolitan campaigns both the NP and the DP promised to defend the fiscal autonomy of the 'substructures' against any efforts by ANC-controlled 'third-tier' central councils to transfer resources away from them.

In Sandton, a previously autonomous municipality, but since

the 1995 election integrated into greater Johannesburg's Eastern Metropolitan Substructure (EMSS), these social tensions between rich and poor have assumed their most dramatic expression. Sandton was established in 1969, initially as a garden city, though its growth in subsequent decades was chiefly attributable to the movement of corporations from Johannesburg's run-down business district to the new municipality's office parks and shopping malls.[75] Burgeoning commercial rates and a generally affluent citizenry enabled the new city's governors to keep residential property taxes low. Householders employed gardeners to trim their roadside verges, required few social services, did not need public transport, and drew their labour from nearby Alexandra. This happy state of affairs for Sandton's office managers and boutique proprietors was obviously difficult to reconcile with the normal social obligations of democracy. Incorporation of Sandton into the Johannesburg municipality brought wider financial responsibilities. As part of a 'substructure' or borough which included working-class communities like Alexandra, Sandton ratepayers would be expected to contribute to a wider range of local government services. In addition, a system of cross-subsidies meant that richer boroughs would help finance better services and infrastructure in poorer parts of Johannesburg.

A new property tax was introduced in the metropolis in 1996; all householders and businesses would have to pay at a rate of 6.45 cents in every rand in new valuation registers. For traditionally undertaxed Sandton residents the new rate scales often represented threefold increases. Twenty-four suburban associations united under the leadership of the Sandton Federation of Ratepayers' Associations (SANFED), which announced a rates boycott and opened a bank account into which ratepayers could make monthly deposits equal to their old taxes plus 20 per cent. By September the boycott was reported to enjoy 80 per cent support and the Liberty Life insurance company, Sandton's biggest firm, announced its affiliation. Boycott partisans also included local leaders of the DP, especially those associated with the free- marketeer, devolutionist Federal Party, which had joined the Democrats after the 1994 general election. DP support for the boycott stemmed from its objections to the authority of 'third-tier' local government generally, and its dislike of the structure of Johannesburg's metropolitan administration in particular. Before the election the DP together with civic and residents' associations (as well as some ANC local activists) favoured a larger number of smaller, and hence more accountable, substructures or boroughs. The DP argued that the 40 per cent of its revenues which the EMSS transferred to the metropolitan authority would be spent mainly on 'a bloated administration and services to mainly white communities' in the other substructures, not on alleviating township poverty.

While it is true that municipal revenues are mainly expended on existing services, which are indeed concentrated in historically white neighbourhoods, and that improving township facilities mainly depends on capital grants from central government (such as the R1.5 billion RDP fund for municipal infrastructure), it seems more likely that most Sandton boycotters were motivated chiefly by resentment of what seemed to them unfairly sudden and steep taxation increases as well as principled objections to cross-subsidisation. Helping to fuel such sentiments was a series of reports of self-serving behaviour by elected and appointed council officials in the Johannesburg vicinity: huge increases in executive salaries and allowances, in certain cases well in excess of government recommendations, and well-reported instances of official extravagance.[76] Few of the ANC's municipal leaders in Johannesburg had succeeded in endearing themselves to the public. A snap survey conducted by *The Star* in November 1996 found that most respondents could identify neither the metropolitan mayor nor the borough leadership.[77] In December 1996 the DP successfully opposed, on grounds of a legal technicality, increases to councillor allowances in the EMSS. Interestingly, the ANC-dominated borough executive was supported by the NP minority. This was an example of a wider trend since 1995 in municipal politics in which ANC councillors found it quite easy to discover common ground with their historical adversaries, the NP, who tended to represent poorer white suburbs – like black neighbourhoods, the beneficiaries of local fiscal redistribution.

Of course, rates increases and tax rebellions were not simply confined to Johannesburg's suburban gentry. The Johannesburg valuation roll included 240,000 properties which had never before been registered, many of them stands in squatter camps as well as more substantial township housing. In the coloured township of Eldorado Park, SOWEJOCA led a series of violent demonstrations in April 1994 in favour of flat rates and free services for poor people as well as pledging its support for the Sandton boycotters, by now engaged in a lengthy, and ultimately fruitless, series of court actions.

Elsewhere in Gauteng there was growing evidence of a widening gulf between the new ANC municipal leadership and civic activism. Though SANCO officials dutifully organised 'Masakhane' door-to-door tours of Alexandra in September to encourage compliance with the new rates, in other places civic movements have been less co-operative. In Tsakane, now part of the new Brakpan municipality, local tax and service payments stood at 10 per cent. In the early 1990s this was not a vicinity in which independent civics had a strong presence; the local ANC branch had tended to absorb activist energies. In January 1997, however, residents were complaining that the ANC had stopped bothering to hold block meetings and councillors never reported back to their wards. Increases in municipal service charges from R30 to R130 for householders had prompted the formation of new residents' associations with names like Simunye ('We are one'). Civic resistance stiffened in 1998 when the council disconnected electricity supplies from defaulters. This action sparked off a consumer boycott and arson attacks on offices and councillors' houses. In October the mayor was assassinated.

In Tembisa–Kempton Park in May 1996, the ANC had to replace its mayor, Ali Tleane, when it was discovered that this former SANCO chairman was not paying for his services. Tleane maintained that to pay anything higher than a flat rate 'would be failing his people'. Subsequently Tleane and his SANCO comrades announced their intention to reconnect electricity and water supplies cut off by the authorities. Delinquent ANC councillors in Khayalami reported by a DP representative, Mike

Waters, provided no such rationalisations; they subsequently paid up their arrears while a joint ANC–NP vote resulted in Waters's suspension. In Benoni, significantly one of the few towns in which power-sharing provisions between the ANC and the NP collapsed, a new Benoni Ratepayers' Protection Association (BRPA) mounted a year-long boycott. Participating white Benoni citizens were reacting to a perception that within the new municipal boundaries they would contribute 95 per cent of the city budget despite having no representation within the council executive. Only R400,000 of the R12 million expended on the Benoni townships of Daveyton and Wattville could be derived from payments from their inhabitants, the BRPA claimed.

By the end of 1996, money owed to municipalities totalled R5.6 billion. Johannesburg itself accounted for nearly R1 billion of this debt, a quarter of it the consequence of the Sandton boycott. Yet, even if local governments were successful in instilling what officials call 'a culture of payment', their finances will remain precarious. Most of the larger cities have more than doubled their populations over the last four years, as a consequence of boundary reconfigurations as well as migration, without any increase in resources. Councils have attempted to cheapen the cost of services they traditionally provide by 'out-sourcing' or privatisation, and such initiatives have often been vigorously contested.

In Tygerberg, outside Cape Town, an NP-dominated council has attempted to institute private rubbish removal, enlisting the support of township entrepreneurs who organise neighbourhood refuse depots and recruiting ANC Youth Leaguers, who were supplied with two new mini-buses so that they could 'monitor' the emptying of dustbins. The scheme was intended to reduce the council wage bill and was predictably opposed by the local branches of the South African Municipal Workers' Union (SAMWU), which branded the council's business partners as community 'sell-outs'. The most protracted municipal privatisation conflict has been in Nelspruit, where the ANC-controlled local government hoped to extend piped water and sanitation to the 90 per cent of its citizenry who are currently without these services, by offering a concession to a consortium of British and French companies. SAMWU opponents of this venture insist that the water will be expensive, that wages paid by the companies will undercut municipal rates, and that the foreign enterprises concerned are 'seeking to dominate world water supplies'.[78]

ANC local government policy-makers believe that the route forward lies in a simplification and centralisation of municipalities to create more efficient authorities, which can eliminate wastage and reduce the scope for middle-class neighbourhood opposition. The new metropolitan 'megacities' will lose their elected 'second tier' (the current substructures), and ward councillors representing very large districts of 100,000 persons will join councillors elected by proportional representation in a single chamber, though ward councillors may choose to establish unpaid, elected, ten-person ward committees. Outside the megacities, municipal boundaries will be rationalised to create fewer, more effective local and district councils.[79] NP officials support the megacity 'in principle',[80] but, predictably, the DP is deeply critical of the policy, partly, doubtless, because it is close to controlling certain boroughs, but also because of its customary antipathy to centralisation. The DP believes that larger city administrations will be less cost-efficient and claims that economies of scale in the provision of services cease when they are administered to more than 650,000 people.[81]

Certainly it is true that under such a system municipal bosses will be less hampered by the obstacles placed in their path by political opponents but it is unlikely that more centralised and bigger municipalities will be any easier to administer. An HSRC-sponsored evaluation of local authorities in Mpumalanga conducted in early 1997 suggests a quite different set of shortcomings in their effective management from those which the proposed reforms attempt to address.[82] The researchers' survey of twelve different municipalities emphasises the significance of the quality of political leadership and depth of political organisation as determinants of effective administration.

This is evident in the report on Middelburg, a medium-sized

former market town in which the economy has been enlivened since 1972 by the establishment of a stainless steel industry. Unusual for its degree of prosperity, this is not the only explanation for the success of its municipal government. Middelburg's local authority boasts one of the highest rates of service payment in the country, and it is the only solvent municipality in Mpumalanga. Since 1994, much of its R40 million capital expenditure has been directed at the Mhluzi township community. Projects include a well-planned RDP housing scheme, the concentration of squatters on a site-and-service area, the expenditure of R24 million on improving township roads, and the provision of new parks and recreational facilities. Some of this success is derived from a sophisticated system for ensuring service payments through prepaid metering and smart cards: consumers have to pay for other services before they can load their cards with electricity credits. Good political relations between the ANC majority and the NP minority within the council have also proved helpful. NP councillors are not driven by party or ideological concerns and most are former ratepayer representatives. Conciliatory politics was fostered between 1994 and 1996 through the Middelburg Informal Development Forum.

ANC political leaders and local government officials also benefit from mutual confidence. The ANC predisposition to trust departmental executives is partly explained by well-conceived affirmative action programmes as well as the capacity of ANC leaders to understand policy technicalities. Generally, ANC councillors are better educated than their peers in other Mpumalanga local authorities – a reflection of Middelburg's unusual concentration of post-secondary training facilities. But what is most distinctive about the ANC in Middelburg's municipal politics is the depth and experience of its organisation. As the researchers note in their report: 'The ANC and the anti-apartheid movement more generally have always been extremely strong and well organised in Middelburg. Indeed it is ironic that this Conservative Party-dominated town was always known by the resistance movement as the "Little Kremlin." It was Middelburg activists that originally brought the Black Consciousness

Movement to the Eastern Transvaal, and when the Soweto riots broke out in 1976, it was in Middelburg that the equivalent occurred. Most indicative, perhaps, is the fact that Middelburg boasts more former exiles and political prisoners than the whole of the rest of Mpumalanga province put together.'[83]

This encouraging scenario in Middelburg is in sharp contrast to the picture drawn in the other case studies. A few examples must suffice. In the trout-fishing tourist centre of Dullstroom, an ANC majority depends heavily on a sympathetic town clerk and an independent councillor for expertise in financial matters. The council functions efficiently enough but is unable to make any decisive contribution to the development of the local economy; this depends mainly on a tourist industry which is wholly white-controlled. Local ANC principals would like to see factories attracted to Dullstroom, an unlikely prospect and one which would be anathema to the weekender fishing fraternity who own most of the town's property. ANC councillors' legitimacy has been uncertain since their refusal to grant municipal wage increases in August 1996 and the consequent emergence of a trade union-based Dullstroom Forum. Councillors depended upon an alliance with the local SANCO branch and thus were at the time of the fieldwork very hesitant to penalise rates defaulters with the severance of services.

In nearby Machadodorp, SANCO also enjoyed considerable success in persuading a divided and insecure group of ANC councillors from taking action against tax boycotters (who also included conservative white ratepayers opposed to cross-subsidisation). Researchers commented on the absence of any civic culture in the township and a mood of 'passive expectation'. ANC leadership weakness was compounded by the personal conflicts which followed the removal of the first ANC mayor, a 'struggle' veteran who could neither read nor write. Other councillors found it difficult to understand the legal language in municipal ordinances. The town's population had doubled in two years, a consequence of an influx of evicted farmworkers, but its capacity to pay officials had declined. In September 1996 municipal salaries had to be funded from an emergency grant by the province.

In Carolina, generally low levels of mobilisation left space open for a series of populist leaders to emerge to challenge the authority of the ANC council. Their operations were facilitated by the ANC's dependence on tumultuous mass meetings as its main channel of communication with its supporters rather than more structured kinds of organisation.

In each of these localities, the ANC's political supremacy was not seriously contested by historically white parties nor were its efforts at governing hampered by recalcitrant officials. Rather, weak municipal governance was the reflection of a political leadership unable, for a variety of reasons, to project authority.

Party performance in the local elections of November 1995 suggested that the forces which would dominate democratic municipalities had not invested much time in preparing locally specific policy programmes. In smaller centres leadership was especially underprepared. In the larger cities, such as Johannesburg, where the ANC has been able to draw upon a politically loyal technocratic elite, relatively qualified municipal party leaders have not fared much better in cultivating a civic culture among their deeply divided citizenry. Given the signals of crossover voting evident in 1995 in Johannesburg and in 1996 in Cape Town, such failures may represent squandered opportunities. Under the fully democratised system of representation which will prevail in the next local elections, the ANC will encounter fewer checks on its authority. Unless this leadership can engender more loyalty and engagement from its constituents, both black and white, South African local government will remain indebted and ineffectual for a long time to come.

5

POLITICAL CORRUPTION

People generally believe there is plenty of political corruption in South Africa. A 1996 IDASA survey found that 46 per cent of its respondents felt that most officials were engaged in corruption: only 6 per cent believed that government was generally clean.[84] In annual surveys undertaken by Transparency International, there are indications that foreign businessmen widely take the view that South African public life is very venal.[85] Corruption has been adopted by the parliamentary opposition as one of the major issues around which it can direct attacks at the government. The ANC itself at Mafikeng in December 1997 reprimanded its own cadres for the dishonesty which the organisation's leadership perceived among ANC members. How fair are these perceptions? Are South African politics and government particularly affected by corruption?

In this chapter I want to address four questions. Is the present South African political environment especially susceptible to corruption? Were previous South African administrations particularly corrupt? What forms has corruption assumed since 1994 and how serious has been its incidence? Is present South African corruption a legacy inherited from the past or is it something new?

Firstly, though, a word or two on definitions and causes. One well-known definition of political corruption is that it is the 'unsanctioned or unscheduled use of public resources for private ends'.[86] Corruption can take the form of 'misperformance or neglect of a recognised duty, or the unwarranted exercise of power, with the motive of gaining some advantage more or less directly personal'.[87] The beneficiaries of corruption need not be greedy individuals: some definitions of corruption also include electoral fraud as well as the rewarding of particular groups by political parties after their accession to office in return for donations or votes – transactive corruption – though this is not necessarily illegal. Political corruption is located within the institutions of government, including legislatures, courts, bureaucracies, municipalities, parastatal corporations and so forth. Very few political systems are completely free from corruption. It is taken to be endemic or systemic when it becomes open and routine, when its workings constitute a parallel set of procedures to those of the proper operations of the bureaucracy. When this happens, public resources can be wasted or lost on a vast scale. For example, in the Philippines during the 1970s, 20 per cent of internal revenue was lost through corruption;[88] in Nigeria estimates for the total of corruption suggest a figure equalling 10 per cent of the GDP;[89] in Zaire similar guesses suggested a proportion of 25 per cent.[90] Some people argue that this kind of diversion of public funds may be beneficial in certain cases,[91] for example those in which the proceeds are expended on productive entrepreneurial activity, but mostly this does not happen.

Analysts of corruption view it as an especial characteristic of government in developing countries. The explanation for this is that in former colonial countries, large-scale centralised bureaucratic administrations are fairly recent and often imposed by outsiders. Hence there may exist a 'wide divergence between the aims, attitudes, and methods of the government and those in societies in which they operate.'[92] In such communities, values which arise from the persistence of kinship, clanship and clientship in social relationships may infuse a bureaucracy from below. Then too, modernisation can enlarge government very quickly, widening its scope of intervention and regulation well beyond the capacity and supply of properly trained people; as such governments' obligations expand, so do the opportunities for corruption. Cases of extreme venality – for example, Nigeria – often coincide with situations in which the state obtains most of its revenues from external sources – customs revenues, payments from offshore oil-extraction companies, etc. – rather than from enfranchised taxpayers. In third world countries, the state is often the major actor in the modern economy – the major employer, the main buyer and the main seller – and this brings more opportunities for misappropriation by its functionaries, especially if the political system is authoritarian.

However, political scientists have recently begun to pay more attention to corruption in rich industrialised and democratic countries, where it seems to be on the rise. Three developments help to explain this: the decentralisation of administration and the delegation of financial authority; the introduction of market values into public administration; and the growing costs of electoral competition, especially because of the predominance of television in party campaigning.[93]

Is South Africa, then, especially susceptible, if we keep these theoretical points in mind? Not especially, I would argue. Firstly, South Africa is not a typical 'developing country'. The state plays a relatively restricted role in the modern economy of South Africa if we compare it with, say, Nigeria's. Since 1994 the government has been trying to stabilise public expenditure and so the state – the bureaucracy – is not becoming any bigger. The state's historical formation was undertaken when the country was dominated politically by a settler minority. Thus it is less likely than in other parts of Africa to be influenced by the persistence of old, pre-industrial cultures of tribute. The South African state depends for a major share of its revenues on various types of personal taxation. This tends to make it more publicly accountable for the way it spends its money than many governments in developing countries.

Democratisation and unification since 1994 may have closed down some opportunities for official spoliation but other potential avenues for corrupt accumulation have opened up. Regionalism has involved a downward delegation of budgetary authority, though this may be compensated for by the dissolution of the homelands in which administrative corruption was sometimes endemic. However, the transfer into regional governments of homeland civil servants may have helped to infect the new system with the patrimonial habits of bantustan officialdom. Although the overall number of civil servants has not changed, senior management has altered with the infusion of new people – often political appointments – and this may have helped to disrupt morale and erode the social restraints which normally keep corruption in check.

The new government is doing new things – channelling resources in different directions – and old rules are often difficult to apply. The government's policy that favours black business 'empowerment' surely makes it vulnerable to charges of favouritism. On the other hand, there is a professed commitment to an ethic of 'transparency' and, certainly, much more official information about the ways in which the government spends its money is available than before. A democratic constitution and the demise of racially and ethnically separated administrations have expanded the area of government open to public scrutiny and inspection. Indeed this is one reason why there seems to be so much more corruption than there used to be.

What about the historical legacy? What did the new government inherit? Government spokesmen contend that modern corruption is mainly a carryover from the past. There is some justification in this point of view. From 1948 ethnic favouritism characterised all civil service recruitment and promotion. Government loans and resources were equally invoked by ethnic and political considerations. On the other hand, these kinds of behaviour may not have been motivated by personal desire for self-enrichment among individual officials, at least not in the 1950s and early 1960s. I have looked at the auditor-general's reports for that period and the number of financial irregularities seems very modest, confined mainly to the Post Office and, to a lesser extent, the departments of Justice, Defence and the Police. Significantly, though, the auditor-general reports stopped routinely detailing 'malfeasances' after 1967.

There is plenty of evidence, however, that as the National Party administration matured it became more degenerate. By the 1980s political corruption was common in both central government and in homeland administrations. It was especially entrenched in those domains of government activity which one might term 'strategic' and which expended secret funds. The 1978 Information Scandal may have forced a change of political leadership but it did not end the large-scale private appropriation of public funds. During the 1980s the Department of Defence spent around R4 billion per annum on secret projects. Although much of this would have been expended on arms procurement, this itself supplied plenty of chances for private profit, with officials setting up ostensibly private companies in foreign countries and awarding themselves comfortable salaries. Besides arms procurement, secret funds were spent on propaganda and subversion, carried out by a variety of front organisations. When one looks at the accounts of these activities one cannot help feeling that in many cases the real purpose of these agencies was simply venal. For example, one military front corporation, African Risk Analysis Consultants, issued to its 49 staff Diners Club cards each with R25,000 limits, presumably for the more incidental expenses of analysing risk.[94] In Namibia, Military Intelligence set up a company, Inter Frama, purportedly to generate income for the UNITA leader, Jonas Savimbi, in Angola; this became a conduit for ivory and mandrax smuggling in which the profits were shared between UNITA and South African Defence Force (SADF) commanders. From 1984 onwards, opposition politicians in parliament argued that the Strategic Fuel Fund, established 20 years previously to stockpile oil, was a vehicle for the private enrichment of its officials.[95]

Quite aside from the mysterious world of covert operations, central government departments had a history of routinised corruption. Especially lucrative fields were prison food supply and textbooks for black schools under the Department of Education and Training (DET). Court cases suggest that contracts for supplying these items were frequently awarded in a nepotistic fashion. The Department of Development Aid (the last in a line of successors to the Native Affairs Department), which channelled development funding to homelands, was a fertile fiefdom for dishonest bureaucrats. It was reckoned by a government commission that several hundred millions of rands had been lost to fraud and nepotism in the 1980s through the awards of contracts to spouses, payments to firms for fictitious projects, and so forth.[96] Homeland governments themselves exhibited grand corruption on a major scale. In the Transkei, independence in 1976 was accompanied by a public takeover of South African property and the subsequent sale at bargain prices of farms, firms and houses to cabinet ministers and their friends. In KwaNdebele, the 1994 Parsons Commission discovered a R1 million kickback to officials for building work which was never done.[97] One member of the KwaNdebele Tender Board, a Mr J. Morgan, managed to secure a contract in 1991 for his own company, Professional Project Services, to supervise the erection of 164 classrooms. Several of these were constructed in the wrong places and many were not built at all; even so, Professional Project Services received a cheque for R105,000 in excess of the original agreement. Meanwhile, Mr Morgan's brother-in-law was the beneficiary of another agreement in which his company, Hata Butle Homes, undertook to supply 200 prefabricated toilets, despite the decision of the Board to award the contract to a firm which submitted a lower estimate. The toilets never arrived at their planned destinations.

Amongst the litany of misdeeds by the Lebowa Tender Board was the purchase, despite objections of three of its members, in return for kickbacks, of cleaning chemicals worth R15 million, enough for seven years' supply to the whole government. A similar deal by Dr G.H. Becker, secretary of the QwaQwa Department of Health, cost about 60 per cent of his department's 1993 budget. The list of such anecdotes is never-ending. It represents chronic or endemic corruption in those spheres, undertaken by senior officials, black and white.

More damaging, often, to public perceptions is routine petty corruption – when members of the public have to undertake dishonest transactions with officials in order to obtain services of one kind or another (or to avoid sanctions). Its incidence probably varied in accordance with the degree of rightlessness of the people seeking benefits or services from officials. In homelands, bribery was prolific in pension departments and in magistrates' courts. In KwaZulu-Natal in the early 1980s, researchers found that headmen and chiefs routinely extorted payments for site permits, workseeker permits and disability grants.[98] More recently the Gauteng Home Truths Commission received 800 submissions concerning the management of public housing between 1976 and 1984. Thousands of people were evicted to make room for tenants who had paid bribes to councillors and officials.[99]

Police bribery was concentrated around the administration of the pass laws and liquor restrictions, but it did not end with the repeal of these laws. In 1995 a survey by the *Sowetan* newspaper found that 67 per cent of its respondents knew that police took bribes, a perception that seems to be based on historical patterns of experience.[100] Amongst white South Africans, though, familiarity with corruption was probably exceptional rather than normal and most often arose from encounters with municipal rather than national state agencies. This does suggest that certain key departments of the administration were fairly clean, for example the Revenue Service.

What shape has corruption assumed since 1994? How serious a problem is it today? A large proportion of the corruption reports which have appeared in newspapers since 1994 are reflections of behavioural patterns inherited from old regimes. Pension fraud is a case in point. One of the most expensive forms of waste was concentrated in the pension bureaucracies which administered grants to black people. Up to R5 billion since 1994 may have been paid out to 'ghosts' and double claimants. The Eastern Cape is especially bad in this respect, though the problem affects even the better-run provinces including Gauteng and the Western Cape. In the Northern Province a review of 95,000 beneficiaries of welfare grants confirmed only 3000 legitimate claimants.[101] The ending of secret budgets to the military and the sharp reduction of defence expenditure have closed down one of the most lucrative seams of venality. Police corruption may have become worse as a consequence, perhaps, of demoralisation and disloyalty to the new government. In 1997, 10,000 policemen (out of a national force of 140,000) were under investigation for charges of bribery, theft, fraud and involvement in crime syndicates. The sale of cars from official depots of recovered stolen vehicles and licensing rackets are two particularly profitable fields of police activity. The falling value of salaries in the Justice Department contributed in the same year to a growth in the incidence of docket loss and the consequent dismissal of charges against suspected criminals. Again, this is not a new problem, as a reading of attorney-general annual reports makes clear, but its evident frequency is accelerating. In 1998, 23 officials were reported to have been accomplices in a scheme which issued and laundered Justice Department cheques worth over R30 million.[102]

But not all the misbehaviour is explicable as the persistence of old bad habits. New kinds of government obligations have supplied fresh opportunities. R1.3 million from the low-cost housing budget in Mpumalanga was used by the province's MECs to renovate their 'state houses'. (Why should such people live in official residences, anyway?) Mpumalanga's environmental affairs MEC was discovered to have filed false expenses claims for an official visit to Disneyworld. In several of the regions, audits have uncovered up to R143 million unaccounted for in the primary-school feeding scheme.[103] Only in the Western Cape, where black business empowerment principles were ignored and the scheme's administration was handed over to an experienced NGO, the Peninsula School Feeding Scheme, has it functioned with complete honesty. Nationwide, 12 MECs have been identified as being accomplices in corrupt practices, mainly in the dishonest or irregular award of tenders.

Credit card abuse seems to be particularly deeply entrenched in the parastatal corporations, some of them new entities like the Independent Broadcasting Authority (IBA), whose managers awarded themselves perks and privileges grandiose even in comparison to those which traditionally prevailed in the senior echelons of the civil service. An investigation of the IBA discovered duplicate claims and payments for single sets of expenses, transfer of IBA funds to private bank accounts, acceptance of gifts by IBA councillors, upgrading of sponsored air tickets at the IBA's expense, claims for travel expenses already paid for by other agencies, free flights and hotel accommodation for spouses and families of councillors, and the use of corporate credit cards for personal shopping.

The overall cost of corruption may be very heavy. In 1997 the firm of accountants Deloitte & Touche suggested that losses caused by public sector fraud and mismanagement could exceed R10 billion that year. This figure, 7 per cent of public expenditure, does suggest a scenario in which corruption has become systemic. Judge William Heath, head of a special investigation unit, announced in August 1998 that 90,000 cases of fraud, maladministration and corruption had been reported so far to his colleagues. Since 1996 Heath's unit had recovered R10 billion of public money, which, he believed, represented 5 per cent of the total lost or embezzled that was 'waiting to be uncovered'.[104]

Is political corruption mainly a legacy from the old regime? A lot of it is, as we have seen. Many of today's reported instances of corruption are the consequence of revelations which have come to light through the various clean-up operations that have been in progress. For example, the Department of Social Welfare has been busy amalgamating 14 different systems, and in the process of creating a centralised data base many false claimants have been identified (though this procedure has also caused lengthy delays in the payment of grants to people who are fully entitled to them). Judge Heath has suggested that public fraud was 'as bad, or even worse, before the [1994] election'.

But there are many new sources of stimulation for corrupt behaviour. These include:

• Non-meritocratic processes of recruitment and promotion inherent in certain kinds of affirmative action. In provincial capitals the numbers of professionally qualified black applicants for senior posts or appointments can be very small, and this may help to explain why at least two regional departments have been at the centre of nepotism scandals. Mpumalanga's Department of Finance employed several kinsfolk of MEC Jacques Modipane, and in the North West the MEC for education prevailed on her deputy director-general to employ the services of her sister as instructing attorney in a court case.

• Tendering principles which favour small businessmen and

community agencies and which require more efficient administration if they are to be handled honestly. One thinks here of subsidies to small building contractors. Job creation programmes
have also been very vulnerable in this respect: at least R1.7 million of Department of Labour funds have been lost on various
labour-intensive road projects supposedly administered by local
committees.[105]

• The increasing shortage of skilled manpower in the public
service especially in its financial control systems. If bureaucracies
become inefficient and delays become routine this supplies
incentives for bribery. The lethargy which seems to affect the
issue of identification documents and visas in the Department of
Home Affairs is a good example of a delay-ridden procedure
which represents an incitement for corruption.

• A range of new sources of public finance, including foreign
development aid. The scandal surrounding the allocation of the
money by the Department of Health to *Sarafina II*, a play promoting AIDs awareness, happened mainly because officials believed
that normal tendering procedures did not apply to donor money
– a resource they had never administered before.

• An ambitious expansion of citizen entitlements to public
resources. Examples include the school-feeding scheme and
housing subsidies.

• The contracting-out of traditional functions of government to
private ventures with political connections. For instance, a private company which had discreet connections with the ANC
Youth League was discovered among the bidders for the construction and management of a juvenile prison.

• The rapid social mobility of much of the new political leadership from situations of material hardship. This seems the kind-
est explanation for the behaviour of Ms Cynthia Maropeng,
deputy speaker of the Mpumalanga legislature and former primary school teacher, who, with the collusion of two other officials, siphoned off more than R700,000 from the funds made
available to the regional ANC by the government for MPs'
allowances.

• Party financing in a newly competitive environment. Fighting

South African elections is expensive. For example, in 1997 IFP leaders claimed they needed R100 million to contest the 1999 election.[106] The ANC treasurer-general, Arnold Stofile, told his audience at Mafikeng in 1997 that donations of R2 million to the ANC had now become customary among black businessmen. In return for this generosity 'we opted for the role of facilitators for black business in the country'. The following year, the former director of the Mpumalanga Parks Board claimed that he and other prominent businessmen in the region had established a secret 'empowerment' network in 1996 to direct funds into the ANC's election kitty after a request from the ANC's national organiser.[107] In KwaZulu-Natal, the IFP accepted donations from illegal casino operators while the provincial government began preparing legislation to regulate the casino industry.

Also potentially harmful is the inconsistency in the attitude of the political leadership. General condemnations of corruption are not always matched by an appropriate attitude to individuals. Justice minister Dullah Omar's welcoming delegation which greeted Allan Boesak at Cape Town airport in 1997 when the former ANC provincial leader returned home to face charges of misappropriating NGO funds is a particularly damaging instance of this. Minister Jay Naidoo's decision to employ disgraced former IBA councillors in his communications office is another. However, all this needs to be considered against a background of aroused public and official recognition of the seriousness of the problem. There are in place a variety of bureaucratic and political measures which have been instituted more recently to check such abuses of power as corruption: the Public Protector's Office, the Office for Serious Economic Offences, the Heath Commission and other civil service investigative units, the rationalisation of records, the register of MPs' interests, the impending executive ethics legislation, and so on. It merits attention that at the level of national political office-holders, the only serious evidence of corruption which has emerged against a member of the government concerned Winnie Madikizela-Mandela, and this may have been one of the factors that led to her dismissal. Another deputy minister, Peter Mokaba, used his credit card for personal expenses while on a foreign trip, but this was to replace the contents of lost luggage.[108] Despite public beliefs that parliamentarians are corrupt, the only specific allegation against an MP concerned an illegal transfer of land in a homeland, which happened before the 1994 election. The really strong signal of a government's determination to root out corruption, though, is when it not merely sacks or suspends a corrupt politician − as has occurred − but when the government recommends or encourages the prosecution of venal elected office-holders. It is a tough test which relatively few administrations as new as this one pass with flying colours.

6

DEMOCRACY IN A
DOMINANT PARTY SYSTEM

Since 1994, South Africa has possessed all the institutions and mechanisms which are normally understood to constitute a fully fledged liberal democracy. These include universal suffrage, based upon proportional representation, for a range of legislatures, national, regional and local; a multiplicity of political parties; a constitutional court which has demonstrated its autonomy from the government in, for example, its review of the first draft of the final Constitution; a Constitution which itself guarantees an extensive range of freedoms, many of them entrenched by a bill of rights; a number of commissions concerned to protect specific kinds of rights, including an Independent Electoral Commission, a Gender Commission and a Human Rights Commission; a Judicial Service Commission which helps to restrain politically partisan court appointments; privately owned newspaper and broadcasting industries; and so on.

Of course, it can be objected that the formal institution of liberal democracy does not mean very much if you have a situation in which representative politics is overwhelmed by one large party and in which the prospects of any alternation of parties in government are pretty remote. If that party is a nationalist movement which broadly represents a racial majority in a society that has a history of racial conflict and racial oppression, and if it represents the formerly oppressed group most closely, it might be argued that its supporters will be fairly uncritical, or undemanding, and that this leaves its leadership scope for plenty of misbehaviour. This is an uncharitable view of the dynamics of the

South African political system but it has some validity. In the 1994 election, on the whole, racial affiliations appeared to coincide with the different ways in which people voted, with two exceptions. These were KwaZulu-Natal, where residence in either a rural community or a substantial town divided African votes between the IFP and the ANC; and the Western Cape, where coloured voters split along class lines, with the ANC taking middle-class votes and the NP finding support among poorer coloured voters.

It is not very likely that things will change very quickly – at least, not to the ANC's disadvantage. Political loyalties among whites may shift. A few liberal suburbanites might switch their affiliations to the ANC, as they were beginning to do in northern Johannesburg in the 1995 local elections and the DP might take over former supporters of the NP. But until opposition parties attract African voters in substantial numbers the ANC will remain dominant. When that happens it is most likely to result from a split in the ANC and I do not think this is a serious prospect in the predictable future. As I have tried to indicate in Chapter 3, the ANC – with all the shortcomings and imperfections of the government notwithstanding – has shifted resources in the direction of its main constituency, the rural poor, and for a substantial number of them life is moderately better, or at least there still remains hope that it will become so shortly. Opinion polls do not indicate bitter disappointment among poor people. At worst they show apathy or resignation which, I suspect – and here again polls are indicative – will turn into stayaways on election day, not votes for the ANC's competitors.[109] The ANC cannot reasonably expect to do any better in the 1999 elections than in 1994. Then, its 63 per cent share of the vote was based on a 90 per cent voter turn-out, uncharacteristically high for any normal election. The ANC would like to do better, it claims. A two-thirds share of the vote would enable it to alter some of the clauses in the Constitution it dislikes, at least in theory. (Whether it would change the Constitution much if it was empowered to do so is another question: it is quite useful having a constitution to blame for not undertaking measures which one's popular following may favour but which may scare off investors and suchlike.) The calls for ANC–IFP mergers which began at the end of 1997 would also enable the ANC to mobilise a two-thirds majority in parliament. Certain ANC leaders believe that given that the IFP and the ANC 'share the same constituency' – peasants and workers – conflict between them 'is not inherent' and 'for two organisations' with such similar goals to compete with each other 'is self-defeating'.[110] It is not a view which has met with universal acceptance either within the ANC or, less surprisingly, the IFP. ANC left-wingers can point to plenty of differences of principle between their movement and the IFP. In 1996 the SACP leader Blade Nzimande, for example, characterised the IFP as 'singularly pro-capitalist, neo-feudal, and undemocratic', objecting to it also because of its federalism.[111] Another influential communist, Jeremy Cronin, responded to merger proposals with the injunction that any future co-operation with the IFP should be 'built on honesty, not historical function'. Such honesty required recognition of Inkatha's record of 'narrow ethnic nationalism' and the identification of its leadership as a 'self-interested ex-Bantustan elite'.[112]

IFP representatives also believe that their organisation embodies distinctive values, including opposition to centralisation, commitment to market-oriented policies, and support for inherited leadership, traditional law and communal land, all of which would be obstacles to a merger with the ANC.[113] It is true that Inkatha ministers have generally co-operated with the ANC as coalition partners and that Inkatha MPs seem to conform with the ANC's notion of the appropriate behaviour for loyal and constructive opposition. But this may be attributable to Inkatha perceptions that as partners in government they enjoy a degree of leverage in protecting their interests and promoting their concerns. Such leverage would disappear if they lost their corporate identity as a separate party. 'Common objectives' and shared 'primary constituencies' notwithstanding,[114] the IFP is likely to remain apart from the ANC, especially on those constitutional issues which some ANC leaders find irksome.

Nor is there much of a serious possibility of a left-wing breakaway, the scenario which was projected in Lester Venter's best-seller, *When Mandela Goes*.[115] COSATU leaders prefer access and influence rather than opposition and exclusion. Workers – those who are employed – have not done so badly in the years since 1994; real wages have increased slightly and, if the new labour laws are implemented effectively, their security and rights will undergo very significant improvements. Opposition parties are likely to become increasingly provincial in character. One can foresee the DP taking over from the NP as the major alternative to the ANC in Gauteng, the United Democratic Movement (UDM) maybe making some headway in the Eastern Cape, and the ANC probably winning control of KwaZulu-Natal with the IFP relegated to the major opposition in that region.

Essentially, with respect to political parties things are not going to change for the foreseeable future. ANC leaders profess to believe, and perhaps really do believe, that the ANC's own internal traditions and procedures strengthen democratic practices. Both Mandela and Mbeki at the ANC's fiftieth conference in 1997 referred to the organisation as the 'parliament of the people'. It is true that delegates on that occasion indicated some willingness to challenge leadership, as in the elections for National Executive members and office-holders, as they have done on previous occasions. It was significant that one of the loudest cheers that Nelson Mandela's speech evoked was raised when he criticised corruption. A speech by the labour minister, Tito Mboweni, suggested that the ANC would invest considerable effort in developing a policy apparatus which would attempt to incorporate a broader range of people in the organisation and its allies in the discussion and planning of policy. Barely six months later Tito Mboweni was transferred to the Reserve Bank and resigned all his policy positions, including his directorship of the ANC policy unit.

But one-party democracy, however sincere in its intentions, has had a history elsewhere of losing its vitality. The ANC's active membership has shrunk,[116] mainly, I suspect, not as a consequence of rank and file disappointment at not being able to attend policy discussions, but rather because politics has become, as it usually does in liberal democracies, less exciting.

What is more important in underpinning the new democracy is not the health of the ANC's internal organisation but rather the state of the institutions of government which should safeguard its principles. The most obvious of these is parliament. Here the ANC's record is a mixed one. Some of the shortcomings of its performance in parliament – such as the mere 15 per cent of the total of parliamentary questions asked by ANC MPs between 1994 and 1996 – were the consequence of inexperience. For many of the MPs, nomination to parliament was an acknowledgement of their liberation track record or their relative status in the movement, and they have found it difficult to adjust to the hard work and tedium which characterise legislative routine. There have also been occasions when ANC parliamentary behaviour has been rather obviously constrained by deference to senior leadership. This was evident in the *Sarafina II* furore when ANC members of the National Assembly portfolio committee on health effectively stifled any criticism of the expenditure by Mrs Nkosazana Zuma's department of European Union funding on the musical. The list system through which MPs hold their seats at the behest of party leadership means that defiance of leadership prescriptions carries heavy penalties, for elected representatives cannot cross the floor, except in the case of constituency-based local councillors. I am not sure that this is such a bad thing at this stage; several African democracies during the 1960s effectively became one-party states before their constitutions changed as a result of floor crossing.[117]

However, it is fair to say that ANC MPs have sometimes demonstrated a willingness to confront the executive arm. This was evident in the hearings on child welfare grants and, more generally, it has been a feature of the conduct of the portfolio committee on defence. Education and justice are two examples of portfolio committees which have worked well with their respective ministers and in these areas MPs have often made decisive contributions to the drafting of particular laws. It is worth recalling that ten years ago, many if not most ANC people had a somewhat dismissive attitude to the formal procedures of 'bourgeois' democracy. With their entry into parliament there is maturing within the ANC a cadre of professional parliamentary politicians. This group can be expected to exercise more and more weight and influence in the future.

ANC political analysts are sceptical of views of the state that perceive it as a neutral instrument, 'perched above society', or alternatively as a socially autonomous 'thing in itself'. Hence they have no hesitation in demanding not merely its political allegiance but also a more profoundly ideological orientation. For the ANC, the state is an expression of class interests and 'the most critical area of contestation among classes'. The state inherited by the Government of National Unity (GNU) was hostile to the aims of national liberation and therefore it could be predicted that 'the old order will resist change both from within and outside the state'. In 1998, as the authors of a discussion paper prepared for an Alliance summit maintained, 'the instruments of the state such as the army, police and judiciary remain largely in the hands of forces that were (and some still are) opposed to social transformation'. A transformation process should entail, 'first and foremost, extending the power of the NLM [National Liberation Movement] over all levers of power: the army, the police, the bureaucracy, intelligence, the judiciary, parastatals, and agencies such as the regulatory bodies, the public broadcaster, the central bank and so on'.[118]

Given the history of a heavily politicised bureaucracy from the inception of NP rule, such reactions may be understandable, but even so the willingness of certain ANC ideologues to blur the boundaries between party and state apparatus is a little alarming. ANC leaders and government spokespeople are very ready to view even legal challenges to their authority as evidence of conspiratorial resistance to transformation. For example, a court summons served on Nelson Mandela represented 'sabotage of democracy' and proof of 'the role played by the courts in frustrating transformation'.[119] Business South Africa's challenge of the legal validity of the Medical Schemes Bill (which was unsuccessful) signalled a 'conspiracy' by 'people bent on frustrating the transformation process', according to a Health Department spokesperson.[120] A speech by Mathole Motshekga described preparations for the ANC's 1999 election campaign as the 'battle plans for the final onslaught against apartheid and the forces of the counter-revolution'; the ANC needed a massive recruitment campaign to restore membership levels before the organisation could hope to 'crush all forces'.[121] If every kind of opposition to government policy is viewed as sinister and subversive – and this did seem to be the perception reflected in Nelson Mandela's speech at the ANC's fiftieth conference, in its characterisation of parliamentary opponents as 'implacable enemies' and of critical lobbying organisations as unpatriotic 'instruments of foreign governments'[122] – then constitutional safeguards will offer limited solace for liberal democrats.

The vigour of institutions like parliament, political parties and local councils as well as the political impartiality of public institutions depends as much on what happens outside and around them as on their inner life. Robert Putnam is an American political scientist who has argued this in an especially sophisticated book about civil society, *Making Democracy Work*.[123] He suggests that certain kinds of associational life – across a range of different kinds of organisations – work-related, leisure-oriented, cultural, or neighbourhood-focused – promote values of trust and inter-dependence within communities, values which predispose people to engage more vigorously with government institutions and, in so doing, render them more responsive and effective. What is crucial to his argument is that the associational life which is critical in the process of making democratic institutions effective, however diverse the purposes of such associations might be, must have a 'horizontal' rather than hierarchical character. The associations themselves – civic bodies, sports clubs, hobby groups, trade unions, charitable agencies, whatever they may be – have to be structured in ways which are relatively egalitarian so that the direction is controlled by their memberships. If they are vertically organised groups, like certain church congregations or, alternatively, criminal gangs, when solidarity flows mainly from patron–client-style relations around an authoritarian or charismatic personality, then associational life does not promote predispositions that favour communal civic engagement. Putnam demonstrates the validity of these contentions by looking at evidence from northern and southern Italy. The relatively more responsive and democratic regional governments of the North are surrounded by lively civil societies, whereas the authoritarian traditions of the South are underpinned and sustained by the hierarchical patronage of the Roman Catholic priesthood and the Mafiosi.

South African civil society is relatively well developed, but it has its vulnerabilities. In the 1980s localised political energies in townships and in even more scattered rural communities were channelled into the formation of neighbourhood associations, or what came to be known generically as the civic movement. These built on longer-established traditions of local bodies which had drawn people to basic bread and butter politics since the beginning of modern urban life at the start of the century, mobilising them around such concerns as high rents, poor services, self-serving behaviour by local officials and similar issues. But the civic movement of the 1980s was unprecedented in its size and scope, for it performed a surrogate function as a vehicle for national liberation politics. This was its strength, but also its weakness, for with the triumph of liberation politics the civics lost many of their best leaders. In any case, with their incorporation into a national movement, the civics lost much of their original concern with localised issues. People in the ANC had mixed feelings about civics, with at least one powerful sentiment suggesting they should be collapsed into ANC branches. The subsequent history of the national civic body, SANCO, formed in 1991, has not been happy, not least because of the tensions and ambivalences which arise from its alliance with the ANC and which saw SANCO candidates standing against ANC candidates in local elections around Johannesburg in 1995. The next chapter will explore the fortunes of SANCO in more detail.

The civic movement was only one constituent of a lively culture of associational life that had developed up to 1994. South Africa, apparently, contained a total of 54,000 non-government and community-based organisations, about one for every 740 people, more than in most developing countries, but relatively fewer than in the United States, which boasted one organisation for every 250 citizens.[124] There are probably fewer today in South Africa, however. As with SANCO, many of these associations depended upon foreign funding ($307 million in 1993)[125] to maintain their activities, though another two-thirds of NGO funding was locally sourced.[126] Since 1994, traditional funders, local and foreign, have either withdrawn their support as a consequence of the cessation of the anti-apartheid struggle or redirected their money to government programmes or the politically prestigious Nelson Mandela Children's Fund. Certain donor agencies, USAID for example, are now committed to supporting only 'programs in support of Pretoria's policies', a position adopted after political attacks on a donation it made to the South African Institute of Race Relations.[127] It is not just organisations with explicitly political concerns that are affected by dwindling resources, however. Charitable bodies, alternative newspapers, adult educational programmes, self-help disabled people's groups, research bodies, HIV education programmes, care for the aged, and human rights organisations such as the Black Sash are all represented within the range of bodies that have either closed down entirely or curtailed most of their previous activities. In addition to their particular functions and concerns, many of these helped to elicit citizenship through volunteer participation.

Of course, powerful, politically assertive and politically independent trade unions are a very substantial guarantee for democracy. Recent comparative historical analysis has suggested that the key variable in explaining the international presence and persistence of democracy is 'the relative size and density of organisation of the working class'.[128] Certainly this seems a more useful hypothesis to apply to the South African case than the rather more traditional emphasis in democratic theory on the democratic susceptibilities of the urban middle class, for in this country the main middle-class community has been historically anti-democratic. It is important and encouraging that South African trade unions continue to grow, and continue to maintain critical and challenging demeanours with respect to government, their status as allies notwithstanding. It is encouraging that several important trade unionists declined to stand for positions on the ANC's National Executive in 1997: this was a convincing signal of their maintained determination to defend their unions' political autonomy. As noted in Chapter 1, some of the key features of the Constitution – proportional representation and a limited-term presidency – may owe their presence to COSATU's introduction of them into the ANC's own constitutional thinking. But trade unions have moved a long way from the idealism and egalitarianism which characterised the early stages of their genesis in the 1970s. The disputes in the Food and Allied Workers' Union over financial mismanagement by the union hierarchy are a symptom of a more general tendency for the movement to become increasingly bureaucratised, professionalised and unresponsive to rank and file concerns. And, quite properly, trade unionists have limited preoccupations, focused on the world of work. They cannot always be depended upon to oppose government encroachments on civil liberties in other spheres.

Civil society is of course more than merely the proliferation of structured forms of collective organisation. It also embraces other institutions which help to promote a politically engaged citizenry. Of these, the press is especially important. Nelson Mandela's censures of the press at the ANC's 1997 conference were disconcerting, but should not be taken as particularly menacing. Even in mature democracies political notables often noisily evince irritation or hostility towards critical journalism. Meanwhile, the legal restrictions on press freedom continue to weaken: in 1998 a landmark court ruling by Mr Justice Hefer made it much easier for newspapers to defend themselves against defamation. The vulnerability of the South African press has more to do with its own shortcomings than the government's attitude towards it. One of the difficulties editors face is that there seems to be a limited public appetite for attentive political journalism. More and more people prefer to get their news in sound-bites from television. The only newspapers with significantly expanding readerships are the few remaining Afrikaans publications. Good local journalism has almost disappeared – very few newspapers supply comprehensive coverage of municipal politics, for example. Newspapers struggle to compete with the growing range of broadcasting and television stations for the advertising revenues which sustain their production. Deregulated airwaves do open up other channels for critical commentary and debate but many of the new stations are strongly entertainment-oriented. It is noticeable that much of the investigative journalism which has recently uncovered major government mistakes or abuses – the Motheo housing contract, or the strange goings-on at the Central Energy Fund – emanates from relatively specialised publications like the *Mail & Guardian* with its tiny circulation, its independent ownership and its restricted advertising base.

It would be all the more a pity if the organisational framework of civil society fell apart at a time when ordinary people's values increasingly seem democratically predisposed. For example, two IDASA surveys asked people if in the event of democracy not working whether they would prefer 'a strong leader who does not have to bother with elections' or, alternatively, whether 'even when things don't work, democracy is always best'. In 1995 only 47 per cent agreed that 'democracy is always best', with 43 per cent favouring a strong leader, whereas by 1997 these proportions had changed, the preference for democracy swelling to 56 per cent and advocacy of strong leadership shrinking to 30 per cent.[129] A recent opinion poll found that just over a quarter of African respondents 'might take part in action with other people to prevent a member of a party they disliked most from living in their neighbourhood', a still unacceptably common predisposition but a substantial reduction from the 50 per cent proportion favouring such action when the same question was asked in 1993.[130] In general, there seems to be a decline in determined political partisanship. Surveys conducted by IDASA between 1994 and 1997 indicated that the proportion of the electorate that strongly identified with the ANC fell from 85 per cent to 56 per cent, suggesting the expansion of a potential 'swing' vote, potentially available to a non-racial opposition.[131] These propensities deserve emphasis at a time when within elite political circles, antipathy to liberalism has become very pervasive.[132]

Despite such reassuring indications of more democratic popular susceptibilities, one should not take the health of South
African civil society for granted. It owes much of its present vitality to the cultural renaissance and social mobilisation which
accompanied the great rebellion of the 1980s, and the social capital which it embodies requires constant replenishment. There are
arenas of public culture which are either supportive or at least
tolerant of democratic politics, but nurturing its institutions must
involve the majority of South African citizens in the active exercise of their civic responsibilities. We can no longer safely leave
such tasks to the heroes and heroines who sacrificed so much in
their dusty township streets to bring about the democratic rights
we enjoy today. A much wider degree of political engagement is
needed to sustain them.

7

THE CIVIC MOVEMENT

Despite an authoritarian state tradition there is plenty of evidence of a lively associational life within black communities over generations. The apartheid state was not totalitarian; its retention of a racially circumscribed democracy as well as its own bureaucratic limitations meant that many areas of social life maintained their autonomy. Black South Africans tended to organise their lives outside the state rather than around it, and much associational life tended to compensate for the state's inattentiveness to their needs rather than seeking control of public resources. Because of its lack of engagement with the state there was no particular reason why organisational life should always reproduce the state's authoritarian character. Colin Bundy has traced the formation in the late nineteenth century of early associations of urban Africans, led by modernising elites, representing freehold landholders, ratepayers, tenants and traders. Though they were dominated by local notables, Bundy shows how these 'Vigilance Associations' were increasingly articulated with a popular constituency through the agency of mass meetings and helped to nurture the popular political base upon which the ANC constructed its political following in the 1950s.[133]

Of course there were rival, less democratic but more charismatic claimants to civic leadership. In Soweto in the 1960s the Sofasonke movement of James Mpanza exploited the prestige of Mpanza's credentials as a 1940s squatter leader to build a political machine which dominated Soweto's official municipal politics for the next two decades. This reproduced much the same hierarchy of 'big-man' politics which had existed in his shanty community.[134] Today, Winnie Madikizela-Mandela's following in the impoverished settlement of Phola Park supplies eloquent testimony to the appeal of highly personalised forms of charismatic authority. 'The Winnie described by the residents of Phola Park is strong and has foiled all attempts to break her spirit. She is the only politician who is accessible to that community at all times. She is their friend in need and in deed. A couple of people used the expression that they shared the same blanket, and ate from the same plate with her.'[135]

We need to know much more about patterns of community mobilisation and organisation before we can confidently assume that they are based upon horizontal strategies of mutual aid as opposed to the dependence of the weak on the apparently strong. But it at least seems reasonable to assume that today's forms of civic engagement have a long history. Though it took on fresh forms in the 1980s it may have incorporated older traditions, some of them democratic, others less so.

Optimistic predictions about South Africa's future prospects for democratic consolidation are frequently justified with reference to the strength of associational life, and in particular the vitality of a national network of local community-based organisations which made such a decisive contribution to the insurrectionary politics of the 1980s.[136] However, the extent to which such civic movements represented an expression of organisational culture that could be separated from nationalist politics was far from clear. Through the 1980s many local bodies were united in a federation, the United Democratic Front (UDF), which, despite its ideological complexity, served in certain respects as an organisational surrogate for the ANC. Many civic activists participated in the ANC's clandestine networks and civics themselves were caught up in nationally orchestrated campaigns. This sense of corporate identity shared by local associations, and engendered by their role in liberation politics, found its institutional expression in the formation of a South African National Civic Organisation shortly after the UDF's dissolution. Though SANCO's brief history does not represent the totality of local associational life in modern South Africa, its troubled progress since its formation is illuminating in any assessment of the prospects for a political culture of civic engagement in South Africa.

SANCO was established in March 1992 at a launching conference in Uitenhage in the Eastern Cape. Plans for a national organisation dated from 1988 when the project was first suggested. A national interim civic structure was established after the formation of a 'watchdog' for the interests of community organisations was discussed at the UDF's disbanding conference in 1991. The new body drew into its fold a total of 2500 local associations distributed between ten regions, which were later consolidated into regions reflecting the new provincial boundaries determined by the 1994 Constitution. During the launching conference delegates argued over the merits of a unitary as opposed to a federal constitution. In the end a centralised form of organisation was chosen despite objections from representatives of the powerful Southern Transvaal federation. This decision reflected a general perception that SANCO's internal arrangements should match the unitary constitutional arrangements which it was hoped the democratic state would assume,[137] as well as a fear that a looser federal body would allow the then National Party government to exploit divisions within the civic movement in its proposals to reform local government.[138] An executive committee was dominated by leaders from the Eastern Cape, who were generally perceived to favour close alignment with the ANC. The constitution adopted at the conference required that local branches should dissolve their own constitutions and refrain from any local negotiations with municipal reform bodies. Similarly, local fundraising should cease: funds would be collected nationally and subsequently allocated to branches. In practice, this has meant that in many cases local civics have had to depend solely on subscriptions and local gifts for their financing; very little money is distributed from the centre.

SANCO leaders insisted at the outset that the new movement should refrain from pledging loyalty to any party. As its president, Moses Mayekiso, put it, SANCO 'should be closer to the trade union movement than political organisations . . . [it] has to be independent of any political organisations . . . we must remain watchdogs for the community.'[139] However, at its November 1993 conference, SANCO resolved to support the ANC in the 1994 general election campaign, though its vice-president, Lechesa Tsenoli, qualified this support: 'we are conscious of the need to co-operate where possible, but we want to retain a culture of being critical.' SANCO would continue, he said, to 'get our cue from local communities and not political organisations'.[140] As a consequence of its participation in the ANC Alliance, SANCO lost an estimated 70 per cent of its leadership to parliament and regional governments.[141] On obtaining public office SANCO leaders had to give up their executive positions. As a consequence, since 1992 SANCO has had three presidents. A newsletter reported in 1995 that three of the most important regions – Western Cape, Eastern Transvaal (Mpumalanga) and Border (Eastern Cape) – were inactive or disrupted as a consequence of such resignations.[142] In 1997 it was decided to allow parliamentarians and local councillors to retain their elected SANCO positions: 'SANCO will as a consequence be better informed about major policy trends.'[143]

By the beginning of 1997 SANCO leaders were complaining of the 'extreme marginalisation of the civic by the ANC'. 'We don't want to be treated simply just as another non-governmental organisation that will be called upon to make submissions at the tail end [of policy formulation].'[144] ANC cabinet ministers, according to SANCO officials, had on occasions told the civic body to obtain permission from the ANC before initiating campaigns and establishing new local branches. In the ANC's view, SANCO should confine itself to the role of a developmental agency and cease competing with the ANC in the task of forging a popular political identity. At a summit held in February 1997 to address the deteriorating relations between the two organisations, SANCO presented a report which referred to 'a looming breakdown of political linkages between SANCO and the ANC at various levels of our organisation'. Examples of this trend included the suspension of SANCO from the ANC Alliance in the Transkei and the closure of SANCO offices by

ANC officials, anti-SANCO propaganda distributed in the Northern Province, and the refusal by the ANC in Port Elizabeth to hold meetings with SANCO leaders. Resolutions calling on SANCO to play a more constructive role and on the ANC to be more communally accountable seemed to persuade SANCO's leaders of the wisdom of reaffirming their support for the ANC at the second national conference some months later.[145]

Despite such warm rhetoric at leadership level it is very evident that SANCO's capacity to influence ANC policy has diminished sharply. This is obvious in the contrast between the leading role it played in the Local Government Negotiating Forum of 1993, which produced the agreements for the constitution of the transitional local authorities, and its effective sidelining in the 'mega-city' debate (see p. 52). At the same time SANCO's submission to the Constitutional Assembly for a radical decentralisation of government helps to illustrate the gulf which had developed between its leaders' thinking and the ANC's policies on municipal government.[146]

SANCO's original conception of its role as a community 'watchdog' echoed the protest culture which had animated the civil movement in the 1980s. One of its first actions in 1992 was a call for a bond (or mortgage) boycott in support of the ANC's 'mass action' campaign, which accompanied the opening of the constitutional negotiations. This was also motivated by the banks' decision to 'redline' certain poor districts, freezing bond programmes within them. Moses Mayekiso promised reprisals against bank and building societies which refused loans; this included occupation of offices and pickets outside them as well as calls for international credit sanctions.[147] Mandela's subsequent disavowal of ANC approval for steps that might endanger future bank co-operation in housing projects[148] may have helped to explain the dispirited response to Mayekiso's exhortations. In any case such an initiative would have only reflected the direct interests of a tiny proportion of SANCO's constituents, those who had purchased their homes.

In 1993 SANCO signed an agreement with the Association of Mortgage Lenders. The rapprochement was short-lived as the banks were reluctant to pay for the salaries, cars and officers of 2000 organisers whom SANCO wanted to administer loans and repayments. As a bank spokesman later put it, 'the banks were not prepared . . . to permit community-based organisations to position themselves as filters between the banks and their clients.'[149] SANCO maintained its stance on bond repayments, effectively ensuring its exclusion from the negotiations around the 1994 National Housing Accord and its non-involvement in the initial stages of the government's 'Masakhane' campaign, the initiative intended to persuade township residents to resume rent and service payments. In June 1996 SANCO threatened 'mass action' against banks unless they halted 75,000 proposed evictions of bond defaulters, citing poor construction and high interest on arrears as a justification for 'selective boycotts'. However, a disappointing popular response helped to prompt SANCO leaders to sign an agreement with the parastatal loan company, Khayalethu Homes: it would end its support for defaulting householders in return for rescheduled repayments. 'If you want to be an instant revolutionary these days and be involved in boycotts, SANCO is no longer a home for you,' declared Mlungisi Hlongwane, SANCO's president.[150] This message was confirmed by Moses Mayekiso: 'Boycotts are yesterday's issues.'[151]

In place of direct protest action, SANCO increasingly characterised its prime function as serving as a key agency in development projects. A strategic document published in 1995 described a programme of local development initiatives which would be executed through partnerships between local government, community representatives and the private sector.[152] SANCO was already involved in 'joint ventures with many companies and organisations who want to be involved in community development initiatives'.[153] Some of these have been on a very large scale indeed. One project in the Eastern Cape which the regional executive has helped to launch planned to invest R147 million so as to improve township roads and water supplies.

Such undertakings are not without dangers, though. In September 1995 the Free State MEC for safety and security was reported to have instructed the police to investigate corruption charges against SANCO, the construction firm Stocks & Stocks and a consultancy. Both the companies had tendered for a R60 million shopping mall in Bloemfontein. The tender board included two regional SANCO officials. Minutes of the SANCO Free State working committee for 13 June recorded a discussion in which concern was expressed that 'Stocks has been treated badly' and that this might jeopardise a R150,000 donation it had promised SANCO. A similar payoff may have been made to a SANCO branch in Vereeniging by another building firm in return for SANCO's 'assisting with marketing of this project'.[154]

Even commercial ventures that are more well-intentioned carry their own risks. At the beginning of 1996, following the example of certain trade unions, SANCO set up an investment organisation, SANCO Investment Holdings (SIH), and Moses Mayekiso resigned from parliament to become its chairman. SIH was established with the help of Liberty Life, which acquired 20 per cent of the equity for R1.5 million. Its intention was to focus on joint ventures with companies with which it would invest in a series of focused areas – privatised state services in the domains of cleaning, catering and security, for example. These would supply vehicles for black-managed small enterprises. SIH plans also included the construction of four entrepreneurial development centres, one of which was opened in the Eastern Cape at the end of the year. SIH was also to operate a funeral scheme, to which SIH's own capital contribution was to be financed through the sale of R30 membership cards to each of SANCO's claimed 1.2 million members. In return members would receive a booklet of discount vouchers, supposedly worth R4000. By mid-1997 only 5000 cards had been sold, and the funeral scheme had already paid out 40 per cent of the funds it had raised through insurance premiums.

SANCO's shift into the business world came under heavy criticism from Moses Mayekiso's younger brother, Mzwanele. In April 1997 reports of fraud and mismanagement of a joint venture by SANCO to sell policies on behalf of an American insurance group underlined the difficulties which the organisation was encountering in its efforts to develop a commercial base.

Mzwanele Mayekiso's publicly expressed reservations led to his expulsion from SANCO. This development provoked the Gauteng provincial branch to threaten secession if he was not reinstated. 'Your handling of Mzwanele Mayekiso's expulsion could have the potential to destroy whatever remnants of the working relationship exist between us and the national leadership.'[155]

Quite apart from considerations arising from its developmental mission, SANCO's business operations were motivated by a financial crisis. At the beginning of 1998, the organisation owed more than R1.3 million. SANCO's treasurer was publicly critical of what he described as 'the mismanagement and irregular financial goings-on in the organisation'. From its inception, SANCO had mainly depended upon external sources for funds: major donors in 1991–2 included USAID and the International Centre for the Swedish Labour Movement.[156] In 1996 USAID ceased funding general administration, and eight staff members were retrenched at national headquarters. Most of its national officials depend on salaries from full-time jobs; its president, Mlungisi Hlongwane, for example, heads a new telecommunications company with its offices in Johannesburg's comfortable northern suburbs. Until January 1997 Hlongwane had served as mayor of the Vaal metropolitan council: his resignation from this post was apparently motivated by the perception that 'there was bound to be a conflict of interest in holding a key position in government and leading an organisation that is supposed to put pressure on local government to ensure that it is accountable and serves the people well'.[157]

Joint ventures may yet sustain the organisation financially as well as give it a certain authority as a 'gatekeeper', governing the entry of private development agencies into black townships. But this is scarcely likely to enhance SANCO's moral stature as a community representative. Trade unions have expressed misgivings about SANCO's bid to take over the provision of 'outsourced' or privatised public services through its SIH operations. Some of its more localised forms of collaboration with private interests may also detract from its support. In Alexandra the local affiliate helps run a housing association, which administers accommodation in unoccupied factory buildings, charging R200 a month for small partitioned sections. SANCO representatives had stepped in to collect and regulate rents after the factory owners started charging R400 a month, to the mainly immigrant tenants. In taking over these functions SANCO also inherited the conflict between landlords and tenants, who now accused it of exploitation. Elsewhere, SANCO branches have held back from becoming embroiled in tenants' movements, thereby leaving open opportunities for rival movements. In the inner-city area of Joubert Park, the Johannesburg Tenants' Association (JOTA) emerged after the general election to organise the occupation of six vacant apartment blocks. Its leader, Moses Moshoeshoe, was a trade unionist and an Actstop veteran, as well as a former member of the ANC's Joubert Park branch executive. JOTA became strongly hostile to SANCO, reflecting antipathy between the national civic and Actstop, an inner-city movement which had opposed the formation of a centralised national civic body. In Soweto's Dobsonville area, local traders were high critical of SANCO's apparent endorsement of a shopping mall development financed by the SANLAM insurance group; despite its claims to be the embodiment of 'people-driven development', the mall supplied no opportunities for small-scale retailers.

SANCO's efforts to redefine a role for itself have included the announcement of 'Operation Mpimpa', as 'a gift to *Tata* Mandela' – an anti-crime drive in which information leading to the arrest and conviction of criminals would earn rewards donated by the 'Business Against Crime' organisation.[158] It seems to have evinced little local interest. In Soweto's Moroka a revival of street committees by a group calling itself Youth Action Against Crime seemed to have no connections with SANCO's operation. In reality, SANCO and the civic movement which it heads have yet to identify a coherent sense of purpose. The Community Development Forums, which were intended to be the socially responsive incubators of RDP projects, seem increasingly to be bypassed in the planning of development projects, especially after the government's emphasis since mid-1996 on efficient 'mass delivery' by large contractors. For SANCO the forums were intended to be the main focus of the civics' local economic development initiatives.

SANCO's voice in local government has been muted despite the large number of former SANCO office-holders who sit as councillors, some of whom stood separately from and in opposition to ANC candidates. Indeed, the insistence of SANCO's leadership during the negotiations over local government reform that 'the future of local government must be decided nationally'[159] may well have discouraged the development of an independent vision among local SANCO activists about the concerns of municipal authorities.

At its 1998 national conference, SANCO resolved once again to support the ANC in the general election of 1999, and moreover pledged its 'unashamed' backing for Thabo Mbeki as Nelson Mandela's successor. Notwithstanding qualificatory language about the possibility of reviewing the alliance with the ANC at some later stage, SANCO's identity as an independent and vital social movement organisation seems increasingly questionable. Mzwanele Mayekiso's comments in an analysis of the civics published in December 1996 reflected the unease felt by at least some of its leaders about the future of the movement. Civics, he argued, were in danger of becoming 'rubber stamp vehicles', driven by political parties with a principal function of merely supplying mass endorsement for conservative notions of development.[160]

Mzwanele Mayekiso's reservations about SANCO's direction seem to have been quite widely shared. In August 1997 Gauteng branches were reported to be threatening a secession if Mayekiso's expulsion was not rescinded. An Interim Johannesburg Civic executive committee assembled itself behind the former Alexandra leader; its members included the ex-Soweto Civic president, Maynard Menu. Later, SANCO officials justified Mayekiso's expulsion on the somewhat technical ground that he had tried to tried to register an affiliated research organisation as a non-profitmaking company without their approval. Mayekiso countered with the accusation that SANCO's leaders were seeking to control his funding and that moreover they had failed to provide membership cards and discount vouchers for the people who had paid fees during the recent membership drive. The formation of a new national civic movement was in the offing, he announced.

Meanwhile, rebellions against SANCO's hierarchy have proliferated. In October 1997 the Transkei SANCO regional leadership announced its secession from the national organisation, citing its dissatisfaction with the organisation's ANC ties, promising to support independent candidates in the 1999 elections and complaining about the 'dropping of the RDP in favour of GEAR'.[161] The Transkeian mutiny came in the wake of a history of conflict between SANCO branches and ANC local councillors who were widely and, in certain cases, justifiably perceived to be very venal indeed. Fanisile Ngayeka, the regional SANCO secretary, claimed that 'many SANCO candidates who were assigned to structures such as local government were blocked by the ANC' – a perception which was quite widespread during the 1995 local elections.

Another source of ANC–SANCO tensions in the Transkei was the conflict between SANCO branches and chiefs. At the end of 1994 CONTRALESA, the organisation of traditional leaders, charged that SANCO members were responsible for expelling certain chiefs and headmen from their districts, occupying tribal authority offices in the Herschel district, and 'bypassing' chiefs by assuming the right to allocate land. SANCO's deputy president in the Border region allowed that SANCO branches were often hostile to headmen, who he claimed had no traditional status, but generally they respected chiefs.[162] The continuing tendency of the ANC to attempt to build its support in this area around chiefly authority would have accentuated SANCO's dissidence.

In January 1998, a third location of potential mutiny became apparent when the Northern Cape region demanded an inquiry into SANCO's finances.

If the national civic organisation disintegrates, what kind of civic movement will it leave in its wake? How lively and resilient is the associational life which is represented in the local organisations that constitute SANCO's affiliates? Are they repositories of civic engagement; do they embody the networks which can promote the habits and values that make for good citizenship? Robert Putnam's work, already cited in Chapter 6, is helpful in supplying a set of criteria which can help us answer these questions. Putnam contends that voluntary associations facilitate good government and economic progress because they reinforce habits of social compromise, the spread of information, mutual trust and collaboration, and an ethic of civic obligation. The more dense and overlapping the social networks in which citizens are involved, the more likely it is that they will co-operate and develop the confidence to engage with government. The values and reflexes produced by associational activity are what Putnam terms 'social capital', and like other forms of capital it accumulates with use. Putnam believes that the networks which generate social capital must be fairly egalitarian. Vertical networks such as those represented in patronage systems are never fully reciprocal in their exchange of benefits or resources. Because of this and their authoritarian dimension, they cannot foster trust and other forms of social capital.

South African civic organisations and their supporters certainly perceived themselves as the expression of 'power in the hands of the people' – the agency through which people demonstrated their 'ability to run their day-to-day lives'. The ideology of the movement was democratic and egalitarian.[163] The secretary of a new SANCO branch in Queenstown, in the Eastern Cape, supplied an eloquent expression of civic virtues when he described the aims of his committee. SANCO 'would be educating citizens on their rights and municipal by-laws affecting them' and it 'would endeavour local government to put a friendly face on Queenstown and make people feel welcome'.[164] However, the local functioning of these organisations has often reflected existing social divisions and inequalities, and local social movements are often built around strong dominant personalities and dependent followings. Fieldwork conducted among yard committees that constituted the base organisational structures of the Alexandra Civic Organisation (ACO) during the 1980s and early

1990s revealed considerable differences in their social dynamics. In one yard the committee in 1990 was dominated by representatives or associates of the descendants of the family which historically owned the stand; these exercised authority through clientalistic relations with their former tenants. In another yard the committee was led by former tenants, but tenants of a landlord who had never lived in the yard and with whom they had never developed any close social attachment: here it was much easier 'for people to organise themselves into a structure based on an ideology of social equality'.[165] Today, there is considerable tension between the ACO and the local ANC branch. ACO members stood as ANC councillor candidates in 1995 but their civic background does not seem to have made them any more communally responsive. In 1997 a researcher was told of a general perception that ward councillors did not bother to attend report-back meetings. ACO officials were, moreover, reluctant to use tried and tested protest tactics against the authorities. 'Yes, ACO can march against the ANC but the problem will be that the ANC has been chosen by us. So we will be marching against ourselves. But the point is there is nothing that is happening. And they [councillors] are not showing us what we were expecting from them.'[166]

Fieldwork in Soweto revealed other organisational characteristics, which at least raise questions about the extent to which local civics represent reservoirs of 'social capital'. In Mzimhlope the local civic was affiliated to the Soweto Civic Association, a township-wide body with 45 branches. Like many other such associations it had no formal membership: everybody in the area was deemed to be a member. It held annual general meetings which were quite well attended but the same executive members tended to be re-elected each year. One of these administered an advice office though residents complained that he was not even-handed, citing as an example his failure to report to the police a suspected murderer known to be a friend of his. In any case he tended simply to note down complaints rather than take any action in response to them. In 1995 the civic did not hold a consultative meeting before preparing a list of its nominees for the

Johannesburg council elections. Young people often spoke dismissively about the civic: apparently its leaders had brushed aside their suggestions about peace proposals in the conflict with Inkatha-aligned workers in a neighbouring hostel.

Soweto civics' links with the ANC and its allies tended to prompt people to use other channels when addressing difficulties in which ANC-linked organisations were involved. For example, people both in Jabavu and Meadowlands relied on the Parent-Teacher Association rather than the civic in disputes concerning the conduct of primary school teachers who were members of the South African Democratic Teachers' Union (SADTU).[167] In 1996, there were other grounds for discontent with the leadership provided by the Soweto Civic Association: its officers had failed to accede to branch requests for reports on the expenditure of R600,000 collected in various fundraising events.[168]

Different kinds of organisation have resulted from successive waves of mobilisation. In Leandra in Mpumalanga, the civic association built its following in the 1980s among the more urbanised residents of the municipal township, Lebohang.[169] The ANC, on the other hand, established its branch among more recent arrivals inhabiting the surrounding squatter settlements, who were at odds with the older residents over the allocation of limited resources. This conflict has been expressed by competition between SANCO and ANC-aligned councillors for leadership positions. In this context, and in many others in which local-level SANCO–ANC rifts appeared in the course of the 1995 local elections, a multiplicity of associations tended to reinforce conflict rather than encouraging communal collaboration through overlapping patterns of mobilisation.

The absence of such conflict, though, may not necessarily imply communal solidarity. A letter in a Middelburg newspaper referred to the complaints of Mhluzi township residents after not obtaining help from SANCO in difficulties with the local council. These difficulties apparently included evictions of rent and payment defaulters. Nor did SANCO concern itself with the plight of new houseowners whose walls had cracked and roofs leaked. SANCO ward meetings were increasingly preoccupied with the ANC's 1999 election campaigning and few people attended them. A new body, the Middelburg Mhluzi Concerned Committee, was gaining adherents.[170] In Springs, SANCO opposition to new service charges imposed by the ANC-dominated town council had resulted in the formation of an alliance with the socially conservative Greater Springs Independent Ratepayers' Association in appealing against Valuation Board decisions.[171]

As such developments indicate, SANCO civics and ANC branches (which are often functionally very similar) do not monopolise local associational life though they often constitute its most conspicuous ingredients. SANCO's inability to fund its operations from membership subscriptions is put into perspective by such financial achievements as R80,000 raised to build a memorial to an Apostolic Church leader in Katlehong; in such initiatives, apparently, 'it is nothing for someone, a wealthy taxi owner, for example, to give a R2000 or R3000 donation'.[172] Church congregations, *stokvels*, burial societies and sports clubs are all potential contributors to the construction of civic communities and in some cases their inner life may resemble more closely the egalitarian ethos which Robert Putnam believes is indispensable in the accumulation of social capital. Certainly, there are impressive instances of *stokvel* groups that supply the basis for collaborative local development projects – self-help housing schemes seem to be a particular focus for such activity.[173]

But whether this micro associational life promotes wider patterns of engagement and broader consciousness of civic identity is at least questionable. Research conducted in Kimberley reflected what seems to be an international characteristic of such kinds of associations: mutual trust and collective responsibility were very evident amongst and between members of *stokvels* but did not extend beyond them, and outsiders tended to be more distrustful towards *stokvel* members. Nor did *stokvel* members have a greater propensity to belong to other organisations than people who did not belong to such groups. The extent to which township associational life is mutually reinforcing and overlapping may be quite limited.[174] Such findings bear out a more general feature of South African associational life. It is in many localities diversified and lively but such local movements are not always incubators of the kinds of beliefs and habits which strengthen democracy. Often they reflect the inequalities of the communities to which they belong and the fierce struggles for scarce resources which take place within them.

8

THE AFRICAN RENAISSANCE

Since its appearance in a speech by Thabo Mbeki in June 1997, the idea of an African Renaissance has increasingly assumed an iconic status in South African public life. Today, references to African regeneration are an almost obligatory feature of any major social gathering. A writers' conference in Cape Town in February 1998 entitled itself 'African Literature in South Africa: Towards a Renaissance'. The guest speaker at a banquet held in Johannesburg in August to honour the businesswomen of the year called for women to assume a key role in the African Renaissance. An adult education workshop in Mafeking was told by the national director of National Adult Basic Education that 'the call to Africa's renewal for an African Renaissance was a call for rebellion'. Gauteng's Crown City, 'the heart of South Africa's coming Silicon Valley', was the setting on 3 May 1998 for 'the African Renaissance show', a three-hour performance by the 'custodians of the legacy of culture' before a 'select' corporate gathering of three thousand 'VIP guests'.

The earliest public reference by a government leader in South Africa to an African Renaissance was in Thabo Mbeki's parliamentary address on 10 June 1997. He reminded his audience of 'the obligation to contribute to the common African continental effort, at last; to achieve an African Renaissance, including the establishment of stable democracies, respect for human rights, an end to violent conflicts, and a better life for all peoples of Africa'.[175] Two months before, in the United States, Mbeki had told the Corporate Council Summit of 'a new miracle' which 'slouches to its birth', an African Renaissance which 'may not be obvious' but which 'is upon us'. 'What we have been talking about', he went on to explain, 'is the establishment of genuine and stable democracies in Africa', democracy supported by a generation 'which has been victim' of the failed systems and violent conflicts of the past. 'It is this generation whose sense of rage guarantees Africa's advance to its renaissance.'[176] By the end of 1997, commitment to an African Renaissance had become a 'strategic objective' incorporated into the programme statements endorsed at the ANC's national conference.[177]

Since then, two visions of an African Renaissance have predominated in the speeches of politicians and other public spokesmen. The first is the idea of modernity. The African Renaissance is something that is going to be brought about by means of fibre-optic cables, liberal democracy and market economics. A fairly typical expression of this view was the kind of rhetoric that accompanied a continental telecommunications conference in Johannesburg in May 1998. 'Global village', the 'information super highway', 'cyberspace' – these were the phrases which were summoned to describe a brave new world in which African citizens would click their way into a new millennium of prosperity and progress.

Such visions are not new, of course. In the 1960s, hydroelectricity was the key element which would install a dynamic motor into the African political economy – power stations coupled with the rational bureaucracy brought about by the vanguard party and nation-building ideology. To be fair, today's modernist vision is rather more plausible. It springs from technological developments which are more accessible to ordinary people, which probably do have greater meaning for their ordinary lives. It is impossible not to be moved by reports such as the story in a newspaper of small cooperatives of South African rural women who through basic computer literacy can now market their pottery, acquire information about farming techniques and teach themselves language and bookkeeping skills. These things are happening, and to those who are affected by them they are powerfully liberating. But we are a long way from such possibilities becoming even remotely within reach of universal experience, in a continent where only about one per cent of its inhabitants have access to a telephone and half of those who do must wait hours for a dialling tone. In the Ivory Coast, one of West Africa's more prosperous countries, of the 4000 computers sold every year only a few hundred are bought by citizens and private businesses; the rest are used by government.

In its South African form, the African Renaissance as described in modernist rhetoric often allies itself with the confidence of being a regional power. At the telecommunications conference mentioned above the relevant minister – perhaps unconsciously – echoed Cecil Rhodes's famous ambition of constructing a communications highway, from Cape Town to Cairo. The Engen oil company, sponsors of a conference on the African Renaissance, and owners of one of the largest networks of petrol stations on the continent, advanced the same vision in their projection of 'an enabling system called The African Dream'. Engen's programme deftly combines commercial interests with pan-African ideals in its intention 'to link the splendours of Africa through a continuous network of Afrikatourism routes from the Cape to Cairo – a route colonialists failed to achieve, but which is within our grasp'.[178] To be fair, it is quite probable that, unlike Rhodes, the authors of this African dream expect the traffic on these highways to be two-way. But this is not always the case. In the opinion of one influential newspaper columnist: 'Africa screams for a brave African nation to step on the plate and lead the continent out of the abyss. South Africa with its economic and political clout is the only country with the ability and the moral capital capable of doing this.'

Nor is this kind of thinking limited to local commentators. As eminent a scholar as Ali Mazrui called in 1996 at a conference in Johannesburg for a 'recolonisation' of Africa, with the establishment of a system of trusteeship that would oversee the affairs of Africa's dysfunctional state system. Such a management function would be undertaken by five of the continent's regional hegemonies, with South Africa presiding over its subcontinental hinterland. Mondli Makhanya, writing three weeks before the

Southern African Development Community (SADC) military intervention in Lesotho in mid-1998, cited this small enclave as but one example 'of countries in Africa which are ripe for recolonisation'. 'South Africa,' he continued, 'as the dominant power on the continent, should begin piecing together a coalition of stable nations which could implement this project.'[179]

Such proposals are still regarded with disfavour by South African politicians, but local businessmen have been less bashful. After South Africa, the continent's second largest gold-producer is Ghana; and its swelling mining sector today features investment by virtually every significant South African mining corporation. Anglo American is now the largest investor in Mali; Gencor, the biggest West African mining operator, is opening mineral deposits in Burkina Faso. And it is not just mining: the South African telecommunications company Telkom is just about to resuscitate the Senegalese telephone system; the retailers Shoprite-Checkers have set up stores throughout the SADC region; Maputo's famous Polana hotel now belongs to the Protea chain. As one travel writer put it as early as 1993, for South Africans Mozambique was becoming 'A paradise – recolonised'. Such power does not necessarily engender popularity or solidarity, though. A man selling T-shirts outside a hotel in Burkina Faso expressed his resentment of the visiting South African football team: 'They are not really Africans, They have their own plane, they bring their own food and water, and they think they are above the rest of us.'

Then there is a second Renaissance language which refers to heritage and legacy, which suggests that the impersonal forces of modern bureaucracies, international markets and electronic technology can somehow be humanised and adapted to African needs. This is a renaissance in which African communities succeed in reconstructing themselves around tradition, legacy and heritage, around the values and relationships which characterised pre-colonial institutions and values. In South Africa in the last few years much of this kind of thinking has focused around the concept of *ubuntu*, the idea of humanness, that people realise their humanity through their interaction with others. *Ubuntu* was first given systematic written exposition in the novels of Jordan

Ngubane, who was over a long career a founder of the ANC Youth League, member of the Liberal Party and professor at Howard University. *Ubuntu*, Ngubane maintained, was the common foundation of all African cultures; in essence it involved 'a consciousness of belonging together'.[180] *Ubuntu* discourses have helped to generate a mini-industry. There are today *ubuntu* consultants, there is even an Ubuntu Institute in Pretoria which arranges seminars on such topics as '*Ubuntu* marketing and public relations' and '*Ubuntu* management'. At the Ubuntu school of philosophy (held at the Rustic Pheasants Nest Restaurant, Tierpoort), the theme in 1997 was 'The After Mandela (AM) factor: Will *ubuntu* see us through?' An HSRC presentation at another such gathering suggests that *ubuntu* is more than simply a set of values governing personal relations; that it represents a subsystem which supplies the foundations for democratic institutions: 'The remnants of the African systems have survived years of colonialism and oppression, and have been preserved by many African societies. Some of the practices can today be found in urban areas where Africans live, namely in townships and white suburbs. One need only drive around on a Sunday afternoon in any urban area in South Africa and observe African people assembled, some dressed in uniforms, discussing matters of mutual concern, applying the system of African democracy in their deliberations and association. Many African men and women belong to structures called *stokvels*, something akin to a credit society . . . Deliberations at their meetings are simple: everyone follows the discussion, resolutions are clear and all participate equally.'[181]

As eminent an authority as Yvonne Mokgoro, a Constitutional Court judge, has argued that *ubuntu* principles could help to shape the future of South African jurisprudence. Key *ubuntu* values such as collectivity, unity and group solidarity could inspire realignment of the adjudication process so as to promote 'peace and harmony between members rather than the adversarial approach in litigation which emphasises retribution'. In a social order constructed around *ubuntu* institutions, law 'is bound to individual duty as opposed to individual rights, demands or entitlement'. In such an order, Mokgoro believes, group interests should prevail over individual rights.[182]

Over the last four decades of post-colonial African experience there have been many other such efforts to recapture and institutionalise pre-colonial social ethics. In Tanzania the government's *ujamaa* philosophy tried to base developmental initiatives around cooperative agricultural production in the villages, assuming that such collective endeavours corresponded with pre-colonial values of sharing. Less equitable or benign were the efforts in Zaire in constructing a state ideology around notions of African authenticity, in which the Mobutu personality cult was substituted as a civil religion in the place of Roman Catholicism – a bizarre amalgamation of African patriarchy combined with the vocabulary of French revolutionary republicanism. Kenneth Kaunda's philosophy of Humanism was a more kindly effort to translate the egalitarian ethos of village life into a modern socialist public policy. In Botswana government spokesmen suggest that the endurance of the pre-colonial *kgotla*, the consensual elders' council, supplies the essential fabric of the country's democratic life and helps to explain the survival of multi-party democracy in the country.

Indeed, there is plenty of evidence to suggest that many social arrangements and the ideas which animate them continue to have more meaning for ordinary people than the bureaucracies introduced by colonial conquerors or the economic ethics promoted by the market economy. In many areas of West Africa, traditional secret societies have reappeared, after a long period of dormancy following their persecution by various colonial administrations. In Sierra Leone the Poro societies were joined by youths upon initiation and provided, through horizontally linked age-sets, a form of communal sanction on chiefs who abused their power. With the collapse of local administration in many parts of the countryside, Poro societies are reassembling. They and traditional occupational brotherhoods have provided the local militias which helped to oust the Koroma military dictatorship. There are plenty of other examples of the resuscitation of traditional networks and their enlistment in democratic causes: the role of spirit mediums in Zimbabwe's Chimurenga or war of liberation, the messianic Naparama movement of Mozambique which fought alongside Frelimo regulars in the war against Renamo, and the Mai Mai guerrillas of the eastern Congo who have fought every Kinshasa government from 1965 until the present. How such forms of associational life can be integrated into structures of government that may perform national developmental functions is a conundrum which continues to haunt African state-makers. Yoweri Museveni's 'no party' democracy is just the latest of a succession of efforts that have tried to address the particularistic and localised nature of conceptions of community in many parts of Africa.

It seems to me that neither of these ideas of Renaissance is particularly plausible. The one modernist vision assumes that technology and markets and even prescriptions of government are neutral or ideologically colourless, whereas they are not. They express relationships of power and domination, and engagement with them need not be empowering. In any case they often assume an administrative capacity in government and other institutions which simply is not present in many parts of the continent. Even in South Africa, which is governed by a more capable administration than many, the limits of what government can manage are rather obvious. This is evident in its achievements as much as its failures. The provision of piped water to two million rural people through public taps represents for the minister of water affairs, Kader Asmal, a 'unique achievement even by world standards'.[183] The hyperbole is understandable in its context, but in fact the achievement is paralleled by the efforts of the Tanzanian administration in the early 1970s and falls well short of what Victorian municipal engineers were installing in British cities a hundred years ago. One should keep in mind also the regression which has featured in the history of many postcolonial African countries. In the Democratic Republic of Congo, for example, the road system is 20 per cent of its extent at independence in 1960; in Ghana it took ten years from 1984 to restore roads to their state in 1957.

To prescribe reconstruction through the reversion to traditional values assumes, first of all, that these are uniformly socially useful; secondly, that they are universally prevalent; and thirdly, that people cannot adjust their beliefs and practices in response to changed circumstances and external sources of inspiration. Looking to the past is all the more tempting in a continental environment in which so many of the institutions introduced through colonialism – infrastructure, bureaucracies, notions of borders and nationality – have disintegrated.

There is nothing wrong with *ubuntu*. The concept expresses a compassionate social etiquette which if everybody adhered to it would make life most agreeable. Reconstructing a political order arranged around collective solidarity rather than civil liberties may be quite difficult, however. In any case, not all traditional belief systems are egalitarian or benign. Of course, what constitutes tradition is always a contested issue, but tradition is often invoked to justify oppression and cruelty. In the end, whether the tradition that is invoked really existed or not is rather an academic question. Tradition is used to justify the persecution of homosexuals in Zimbabwe and many other places; tradition is used to defend the absence of democratic representation in Swaziland as well as the extraordinary royal investment corporation, the Tibiyo Taka Nqwana; tradition is used to justify the minor status of Zimbabwean women; tradition is employed whenever African rulers arrogate power and resources to themselves and their clients.

In any case, the invocation of tradition ignores the extent to which Africa has changed. Today half of the continent's population live in towns, not in villages or homesteads, but in circumstances in which traditional ideas of reciprocity and social responsibility are very difficult to sustain. By the first decade of the twenty-first century it is likely that most Africans will speak English, not just as an occasional medium of communication in the workplace but as the language of everyday life. Today television has become accessible to even the poorest urban communities. Transcontinental patterns of trade and migration are also beginning to reshape African notions of distance, locality and community – think of the ten thousand Nigerians who live and work in Johannesburg, or the tens of thousands of Congolese who keep South Africa's public health system functioning, or the street markets in Johannesburg which sell Ethiopian prayer scrolls to wealthy suburbanites. Consider, too, the case of the Samburu warriors of Kenya, a pastoral people whose local economy depended upon cattle herding and whose homesteads subsisted on cash incomes of a few hundred rands a year – until 1992, that is, when the age-sets began to be recruited into a United Nations peacekeeping force and dispatched to Bosnia, to earn $4500 a month, later to be invested in bottlestores and teashops. Here we see a new entrepreneurial elite shaking loose the community bonds of a society built around cattle and grass.

Not that the capacity of people to embrace new ideas need be corrupting or destructive. East of Nairobi is the Machakos district, described by a British colonial soil inspector in the 1930s as a dustbowl, 'an appalling example of environmental degradation . . . in which the inhabitants are rapidly drifting to a state of hopeless and miserable poverty and their land to a parched desert of rocks and stones and sand'. Since then the population has risen five times and yet today the landscape is a green garden of fertility and industry in which farmers export mangoes to the Middle East, coffee to the breakfast tables of Europe, and most of the tomatoes consumed in Nairobi. The change came about through the experiences of African soldiers who served in India during the Second World War and returned home inspired by the terraced hillsides they had fought across in the Eastern theatre and determined to imitate the technique locally. Although terracing had been advocated and implemented by British colonial bureaucracies in more than a dozen African colonies, the difference was that in Kenya the technique was adopted by local people rather than imposed upon them and adapted to their environmental and social needs. In the Machakos experience women have played an increasingly important role in agricultural innovation.

This is another point that deserves emphasis: how over the last century in African communities, again and again, the division of labour and the relationship between genders and generations change, and with these changes there are shifts in values, ideas, knowledge and power. In such a context, trying to reconstruct tradition is misguided: there is no such thing as one fixed set of traditions. Even if there were, they might not be very useful.

Contemporary African philosophers such as Cameroon's Marcien Towa and Benin's Paulin Houtondji concur that 'the traditional values of African societies cannot justly be characterized as philosophy in the sense of a systematic methodology applied to defined areas of analysis such as logic or ethics'. In this vein, Kwasi Wiredu of the University of Ghana writes disparagingly of 'the spectacle of otherwise enlightened Africans pouring libations to the spirits of their ancestors . . . That our departed ancestors continue to hover around in some rarefied form ready now and then to take a sip of the ceremonial schnapps is a proposition that I have never heard rationally defended.'[184]

In South Africa public calls for an African Renaissance are quite rightly understood to imply a process of political, economic and cultural re-engagement with the rest of the continent, as well as a process of recognition of South Africa's identity as African. What being African means has become a key preoccupation of Renaissance commentators. For Thabo Mbeki, Africans are those people who view the continent as their home in the fullest emotional sense. 'I am an African,' he told the Constitutional Assembly on 8 May 1996. 'I owe my being to the Khoi and San . . . I am formed of the migrants who left Europe to find a new home on our native land . . . I am the grandchild of the warrior men and women that Hintsa and Sekhukhune led . . . I am the grandchild who lays fresh flowers on the Boer graves at St Helena.' For other authorities, however, finding one's home in Africa means more than a sense of shared history. 'Declaring oneself an African', the University of the Witwatersrand's Professor William Makgoba maintains, is not 'simply being located in Africa'. Makgoba believes that whereas there is 'no need to entertain a genetic cause of African thought', amongst all authentically African cultures 'there are profound and prolonged areas of convergence' and 'there is something specific and particular about African thought processes'. These, he thinks, include *ubuntu*, 'looking at things holistically, looking for meaning and symbolism in phenomena, consensus or group identity' and 'the inclusion of the unseen or spiritual dimension of life'.[185] Presumably, those who do not share such 'thought processes' are not African.

The West African sociologist Kwesi Kwaa Prah, now based at the University of the Western Cape, is even less shy of essentialist conceptions of African identity: 'the fact that most South Africans or people of African historical or cultural descent are black is only one characteristic, a bonus which generalizes and typifies Africans'. However, while he argues that 'colour has become an easy and fortunate identifying attribute of most people who regard themselves as African', Prah insists that 'culture, history and attachment to these and consciousness of identity and not skin colour, primarily define the African'.[186] Nevertheless, in practice cultural conceptions of African identity are often accompanied by a racial emphasis. The Gauteng premier, Mathole Motshekga, in addressing an African Renaissance conference in Midrand, took as his theme the concept of *kara*, an idea, he said, that was to be found in many African languages. *Kara*, Motshekga told his audience, was a root word for the name of God, the same God who made the sun. 'There is therefore a close relationship between the way Africans saw God, the creator of all things, and the life-giving force of light we call sunlight. African people are people baked by the sun, while *kara* is a word for divinity.'[187]

Proclamations of an African Renaissance are neither original nor new. As early as 1937, Nnamdi Azikiwe, the future president of Nigeria, published his intellectual manifesto, *Renascent Africa*.[188] Azikiwe was one of the first African leaders to recognise the political opportunities represented by generational consciousness. His contention 'that youth is the sine qua non in the political evolution of the various nations of the world' inspired a legion of youth movements which assumed the leadership of nationalist organisations across the continent, from Cairo to Johannesburg. Leonard Barnes's *African Renaissance*,[189] written by a former British civil servant shortly before the victory of revolutionary peasant insurgencies in Portuguese Africa, perceived the best prospects for an African rebirth in a rurally oriented African socialism. His prescriptions included disengagement from world markets, planned village settlement, and limits on urbanisation to counter 'the menace of the towns'. In this vision Sékou Touré's Guinea offered the most instructive lessons of 'peasant truth'. Nearer to home, in Hammanskraal outside Pretoria a Black Renaissance Convention[190] assembled in 1974 'to re-examine our cultural heritage in the light of modern and contemporary developments'. The intellectual genealogy of Thabo Mbeki's deployment of the Renaissance concept may also include a speech by Malaysia's prime minister, Mahathir Mohamad, delivered at the beginning of 1997, shortly before Mbeki's visit to the Federation, in which the Malaysian leader referred to an 'Asian Renaissance' constructed on the foundations of information technology and Islamic social principles.

Calls for an African Renaissance punctuate the history of the continent's intellectual community. Today, however, such exhortations may have a much wider and more socially profound impact. What is historically unprecedented about Mbeki's optimistic vision is that it is reinforced not just by the authority of the South African state but also by the corporate culture of Africa's most powerful economy. A journalist's description of an SABC-sponsored 'Celebration of the African Renaissance' underscores this point. 'From the moment one walked into the expansive foyer illuminated by a score of flaming torches on tripods, you could feel you were in for a different experience. The atmosphere was exotic, understated and quintessentially African, and the music was quiet, rhythmic and soothing . . . Each table had as its centrepiece an African footstool, depicting tradition. An arrangement of thornbush and porcupine quills conveyed Africa's rustic nature and the wealth of its animal life. A giant protea in the centre of the quills and thorns symbolised the beauty of Africa, according to a page headed "Table detail." The banquet hall was flanked by huge murals of San rock-paintings with cubes of African thornbush signifying "A new Africa dawning."'[191]

After a 'multimedia' stage show, those in attendance watched a live television transmission of Thabo Mbeki's latest oration. On departure each guest received a bound copy of Mbeki's seminal speeches encased in a wooden box in the shape of a book with a hinged cover. Quite aside from the aesthetic vulgarity of these arrangements, this final conferment of canonical authority on Mbeki's texts is a little alarming. Personality cults, no matter how benign, are an African tradition quite difficult to reconcile with the tenets of democracy. Notwithstanding Mbeki's grounding of his Renaissance concept in democratic values, culturally specific projections of African regeneration can have, as we have seen, an authoritarian dimension: Mokgoro's communal *ubuntu* jurisprudence, however humane its intention, is one example of this tendency.

What is one to make of Mbeki's Renaissance? It is striking how within a very short passage of time it has assumed the status of a collective discourse, articulating a sense of social purpose within South Africa's new intellectual and business leadership. Its advent follows four years of very rapid expansion of a new entrepreneurial and managerial class. Evidence of this trend includes the accelerating black share of market capitalisation on the Johannesburg Stock Exchange, from 11 black-owned companies worth R4.6 billion in September 1995 to 28 companies representing a capitalisation of R66.7 billion – 10 per cent of the total shareholdings listed – in February 1998.[192] In the civil service by 1996, Africans filled 30 per cent of management posts compared with only 2 per cent in 1994.[193] Between 1994 and 1997, the number of black South Africans earning more than R5000 a month jumped by 52 per cent, from 310,000 to 472,000.[194]

Significantly, the other major political advocate of continental regeneration, the Ugandan president, Yoweri Museveni, has constructed his programme around market economics, regional integration and the 'restoration of sovereignty' to African 'wealth producers'.[195] It remains to be seen whether a new class of African proprietors will be more predisposed than previous generations of nationalist leadership to become infused with the 'democratic rage' against corruption and tyranny that Mbeki attributes to it. The Afrocentrist historical nostalgia which characterises many of the efforts to develop the Renaissance project – the key authorities in this context are Ivan van Sertima and Cheikh Anta Diop – may be rather more inviting for members of the new 'patriotic bourgeoisie' than the conceptual difficulties that arise from

Mbeki's challenge to 'put behind us the notions of democracy and human rights as peculiarly Western.'[196] All too easily the idea could become debased into a series of self-congratulatory maxims in which the recollection of the African identity of ancient civilisations – 'the presence of melanin in the skin fragments of Egyptian mummies'[197] – becomes the founding myth for a new imagined community in which racial sentiment rather than political principle is the animating idea.

9

THABO MBEKI: MANDELA'S SUCCESSOR

In new democracies the quality of political leadership matters more than in established political systems, however carefully scripted the constitutional safeguards may be against the abuse of power. Institutions are still fluid and susceptible to being shaped by dominant personalities. One of the most common questions asked about our political affairs is how well South Africa will be governed under a Mbeki presidency. Certainly the country's present international status owes much to the moral stature enjoyed by President Mandela as well as the evident affection which he inspires amongst South African citizens regardless of their political affiliations or social circumstances. Mandela's almost assured successor may well in future years accumulate a similar degree of charismatic authority but today, even among his admirers, he is respected rather than loved.

In contrast to the man whom he will succeed as head of state in 1999, not much is publicly known about Thabo Mbeki. To be sure, the basic details of his career are easy enough to recite. Born in the Transkei in 1942, he belonged to an important ANC household, the third-generation representative of a lineage drawn from a 'typically "progressive" or modernising peasant family characteristic of the region at the turn of the century'.[198] His grandfather, Fkelewu, was a Presbyterian convert, salaried headman and a peasant farmer; his father, Govan, a prominent member of the Communist Party and an influential journalist. Thabo was politically active from the age of 14 when he joined the Youth League (two years before the normal age of entry); he helped establish an African Students' Association in South Africa while taking a correspondence degree course from London University; and he left South Africa in 1962 after a brief spell in detention. Three years later he graduated from the university of Sussex with an economics MA before working in the ANC's London office and undertaking a brief stint of military instruction in the Soviet Union. From 1971 he served as assistant secretary to the ANC's Revolutionary Council and subsequently represented the ANC in Nigeria, Botswana and Swaziland. In 1975, he became Oliver Tambo's political secretary and speech-writer, he was elected to the ANC's National Executive in 1978, became director of information in 1984, and head of the organisation's international affairs department in 1989. Four years later, in August 1993, he was appointed to the national chairmanship, a honorary position created two years earlier for the ailing Oliver Tambo, who died in April 1993.

During the CODESA talks between the De Klerk government and the ANC, Mbeki participated as a member of the ANC team in the working group which considered transitional government arrangements — a relatively low-profile contribution. He played a more decisive transition role in his successful efforts to persuade General Constand Viljoen to bring his following, the Freedom Front, into the settlement. In 1994, his assumption of the deputy presidency more or less confirmed his status as Mandela's successor. In contrast to the public scrutiny directed at Nelson Mandela's domestic circumstances, Thabo Mbeki's family life is kept firmly private. Mrs Zanele Mbeki works well out of the limelight, running the Women's Rural Development Bank, an extremely effective NGO which supplies loans to help rural women start up businesses. In this she draws upon her exile experience as an administrator for the United Nation High Commission for Refugees in Lusaka. His one child, Monwabisi, a son born from a youthful love affair, was last seen by members of Mbeki's family in 1981; he subsequently disappeared, though his mother later received reports from his friends, who told her of their meeting him in a military camp in Tanzania.

Filling in the gaps in this curriculum vitae is not easy. Mbeki himself eschews confessional statements. As one interviewer noted in 1993, 'Thabo Mbeki has great difficulty talking about himself . . . and prefers to talk about the ANC instead, and even then downplays the role he has filled.'[199] Some of his self-contained reticence probably stems from an upbringing in which family relations were very disrupted. As Mbeki told one journalist in 1994, because of his parents' political commitments 'we did not grow up at home. From the ages of six and seven we were dispatched to relatives and friends . . . I can count on one hand the political discussions I've had with my father.'[200] Though Mbeki occupied a key position at the ANC's nerve-centre of strategic decision-making from the late 1970s onwards, as a firm subscriber to the ANC's traditional etiquette of 'collective leadership' he has never claimed personal responsibility for particular developments. He is generally credited with inventing the 'Make South Africa ungovernable' slogan popularised by the ANC in the early 1980s. Conversely, and more reassuringly to white South Africans, he is believed to have been one of the strongest advocates of negotiated settlement at the end of the decade. One encounter with Afrikaner intellectuals in 1988 even earned him a censure from the ANC's National Working Committee for failing to obtain appropriate authority before the meeting.[201] When delegations representing various white South African elites started travelling in the 1980s to Lusaka to meet the ANC, it was Mbeki who was their most prominent host. Well before his return to the country Mbeki had probably become the best-known and most receptive black South African politician among businessmen and mainstream journalists. Though Peter Mokaba, the former Youth League president (and in that capacity, one of Mbeki's key supporters in the succession contest), has referred to Mbeki's guerrilla accomplishments, the deputy president is more commonly associated with the exile ANC's diplomatic efforts as well as its increasing commitment during the 1980s to social, if not liberal, democracy.

Like most ambitious ANC exiles of his generation, Mbeki joined the Communist Party and even gained election to its Politburo. In 1978 Mbeki's ideological affinities were well on the left of the ANC's political spectrum. In one address to a Canadian conference he referred to 'black capitalism' as 'parasitic' and 'senile', historically obsolete, 'without any extenuating circumstances to excuse its existence'.[202] His active involvement in the Party's affairs, however, stopped long before his return to South Africa. But he has remained friendly with individuals in the party: Essop Pahad, for example, now the deputy minister responsible for the administration of Mbeki's office and his liaison with the ANC's parliamentary caucus, is a veteran communist, but this should not be taken to signify anything about Mbeki's ideological predispositions. In 1994 leading communists, including Joe Slovo, were known to favour Cyril Ramaphosa's appointment to the position of deputy president, as did Nelson Mandela. Significantly, in 1996 Mbeki became the first major contemporary ANC leader to speculate publicly about the possibility that with the achievement of 'a more normal society', out of the 'broad movement' that the ANC represented would emerge different parties, with liberals and socialists going their separate ways.

How can one explain Mbeki's ascendancy in the organisation? In a characteristically perceptive aside in an interview given in 1995, he observed, 'I don't have constituencies.' Though journalists like to speculate about divisions within the ANC based either on ideological factions – communists or Africanists, for example – or different trajectories of struggle experience – exiles, prisoners, Mass Democratic Movement – these supply a misleadingly simple view of the organisation's internal politics. Communist notables can be counted among Mbeki's most prominent critics and can be identified as his strongest allies. Sydney Mufamadi, the minister of safety and security, and Sam Shilowa, general secretary of the trade union COSATU, are two important personalities in the latter category. Nor is the ANC's aspirant 'patriotic bourgeoisie' camp uniform in its attitudes to Thabo Mbeki. Peter Mokaba is a Mbeki associate but Cyril Ramaphosa and Tokyo Sexwale are two former rivals who, once outmanoeuvred in the leadership stakes, have redirected their energies towards business.[203] Part of his strength is that Mbeki does not represent a particular ideological predisposition in the ANC.

Mbeki's status as a successor leader was evident a long time ago: in the guerrilla training camps his name was coupled with that of his old Lovedale classmate, Chris Hani, as the two outstanding leaders of the younger generation. Generational seniority remains an important consideration in the ANC's pecking order. Mbeki's position as ANC national chairman was decided in 1993 not by delegates at a conference but rather by a meeting of the National Working Committee. By the end of the ANC's exile, aside from Tambo and Mandela, Mbeki was probably the most familiar ANC personality to the broader public inside South Africa as well as to external audiences. Mbeki probably did not need 'constituencies' to secure delegate support at the 1994 ANC conference, though the public backing he received from Peter Mokaba, a key 'internal' leader of the 1980s, did not harm him. Winnie Madikizela-Mandela's antipathy to his rival, Cyril Ramaphosa, ensured the support of the ANC Women's League at the 1994 conference. In the 1997 leadership elections, Mbeki faced no opponents: his was the only nomination for the post of ANC president, an isolated carry-over from a more deferential past when most ANC leadership positions were uncontested.

The position of deputy president of South Africa in the first ANC government had a special significance, given Mandela's professed intention to serve only one term and given the president's own decision to delegate considerable executive authority to his deputy. As the chairperson of most cabinet meetings, Thabo Mbeki has effectively been responsible for the routine administration of government since 1994. As Mandela explained to an audience in Singapore in early 1997, 'I am doing less and less work. That is being done by the present Deputy President.'[204] Nor have Mbeki's responsibilities been confined to day-to-day supervision of the executive. Since 1994 he has increasingly become the main arbiter of policy issues and successive cabinet appointments have testified to his decisive role in government. The dissolution of the RDP office in 1996 and the transfer of many of its functions to the deputy president's burgeoning staff was another important signal of his consolidating authority. This should not be exaggerated, though. Mandela's first cabinet included several strong independent personalities who were not especially intimate with Mbeki – Mac Maharaj and Tito Mboweni were examples. Ministers who have disagreed with him in public have retained authority: Dullah Omar's clash with Mbeki over the issue of secret hearings at the Truth and Reconciliation Commission for senior officials from the old regime is a case in point.

To an extent, the future prospects of South Africa under a Mbeki presidency can be calculated from the track record of the Mandela administration. Which particular features should be associated with Mbeki's influence? Not, one suspects, its commitment to liberal principles. Mbeki was not one of the architects of South Africa's constitutional dispensation. He is known to dislike especially its federal dimensions. His occasional attacks on the press also demonstrate a prickliness which some critics interpret as authoritarian. Attacks on the liberal press's 'counter-revolutionary' activities arouse understandable alarm, which is not adequately assuaged by Mbeki's protestations that 'the problem is not what is being written but what is not being written'. Mbeki may be less than enthusiastic about the constitutional two-term limitation on the presidency, though any efforts to modify it will encounter strong opposition from COSATU, an early advocate of its inclusion.

As deputy president, his key achievement has been in setting a coherent policy agenda. Depending on one's perspective he probably deserves the principal credit or the main blame for the government's fiscally conservative macroeconomic policies.[205] Though the drafting of the GEAR document was undertaken by a team of economists working with the minister of finance, the deputy president's office was closely involved in the discussion of early drafts, well before the programme was shown to the ANC's executive, the cabinet or even Nelson Mandela. The task of justifying and defending GEAR in public has normally been undertaken by the minister of finance, Trevor Manuel, and the minister of trade and industry, Alec Erwin, though it was Mandela himself who appeared at the 1997 COSATU conference to confront labour's criticisms of policy. Mbeki's public statements on GEAR have been less conspicuous, though he has spoken in favour of the programme in press and television interviews – his preferred method of public communication. At the SACP's tenth congress, in July 1998, though, following an angry repudiation of GEAR critics by Mandela, Mbeki lectured the assembled delegates on the dangers of 'fake revolutionary posturing', accusing party leaders of trying to boost their following 'on the basis of scavenging on the carcass of a savaged ANC'.[206] GEAR's contents certainly reflect Mbeki's convictions about the imperatives of good government but it is probably still the case that in the popular mind he is not directly associated with the programme. If the ANC is compelled by its own following and its allies to shift course on macroeconomic policies, his own authority within the movement and among its traditional constituency will be undiminished. At this stage in his career, deflecting responsibility for contentious policies may be interpreted as canny politics but sooner or later, as president, Mbeki will have to defend unpopular executive decisions in front of a hostile audience. As he himself has noted, 'if you believe that the positions you have taken are correct, you have to stand up and say they are correct.'

To date, however, leading from the front in such a fashion has not been Thabo Mbeki's perceived main strength. In a 1995 interview Nelson Mandela conceded that Thabo Mbeki was not at his best in dealing with 'day to day problems'. Some 'of our own people' thought that Mbeki was too indecisive, he conceded.[207] Mandela was reacting to Mbeki's awkward handling of Winnie Mandela's resignation from her deputy ministership as well as the attempt by Mbeki's legal adviser to exonerate Dr Allan Boesak from corruption charges, both issues in which Mbeki's predisposition to compromise rather than confront was well to the fore. Like his mentor, Oliver Tambo, Thabo Mbeki's reflexive inclination seems to be to placate potential troublemakers and keep them within the fold, until at least their supporters can be won over. As Mandela conceded on another occasion, 'He can be diplomatic to the point where many people regard him as weak.' The high premium which Mbeki and other former exile leaders in the ANC place on organisational cohesion and unity is understandable but it has a less beneficial effect when it is applied to the business of government.

Not that Mbeki is incapable of acting firmly against opponents. The expulsion from the government and from the ANC's ranks of Bantu Holomisa, the deputy minister of environmental affairs and former head of Transkei, was convincing evidence of the dangers of clashing publicly with the deputy president. The singularity of Holomisa's situation, though, was that as a latecomer within the ANC he had no support network within the organisation, his popularity with delegates to the 1994 conference notwithstanding. Though Thabo Mbeki has been careful to maintain courteous public relations with Winnie Madikizela-Mandela he has also been generally supportive of some of her leading critics: amongst these is Mavivi Myakayaka Manzini, who in 1996 replaced Essop Pahad as the deputy president's parliamentary counsellor after Pahad's promotion to a deputy ministership. The experience of holding office may have helped Mbeki to develop a more confident way of dealing with open opposition. This was manifest in February 1997 at the ANC Free State conference, which was bitterly divided between supporters of the deposed premier, Patrick Lekota, and his opponents. 'The ANC', Mbeki reminded his audience, 'is a voluntary organisation. If you do not agree with majority decisions, then you are free voluntarily to leave as you are to join.'[208] Sometimes, though, his growing confidence in open forums can be intimidating. Parliamentarians complain that they feel increasingly reluctant to challenge the executive. At one ANC caucus meeting in 1997, Barbara Hogan kept prefacing her remarks with the phrase that she 'did not want to cause any trouble'. To his credit Mbeki intervened and said he was worried that she felt it necessary to say this. Was there, he asked, a more general feeling that the ANC leadership did not welcome dissent? 'Yes-s-s,' the MPs whispered in chorus.[209]

Thabo Mbeki's normal leadership style is that of a political manager, not a charismatic populist. As one commentator put it, 'he works behind the scenes, patching together alliances of disparate ANC factions to produce a power base.'[210] There is much to be said for such leadership, especially in a context in which the

ANC has to please so many different constituencies, and also when it is aided, as in Mbeki's case, by an affable personal manner and a convincing television presence, an increasingly important factor in South African politics. Mbeki's skills as a negotiator, working behind the scenes, deserve much of the credit for the decline in political violence in KwaZulu-Natal after 1994. The problem with the behind-the-scenes managerial approach, though, is that the ANC as an organisation is not particularly susceptible to management. This has been evident in the resistance of provincial organisations to electing leaders supported by higher authority as well as the difficulties the ANC leadership encountered in securing delegate support for Jacob Zuma, ANC leader in KwaZulu-Natal, in the December 1997 conference elections to the position of ANC deputy president. Zuma is a friend of Mbeki but his candidature for the election probably owed more to his work with Mbeki in the KwaZulu-Natal peacemaking process. The choice of Zuma was also a significant indicator of the Mbeki leadership style. Zuma has the reputation for being a highly effective negotiator and a skilful strategist. Amongst top-echelon ANC leaders, particularly those from exile, he was especially trusted and liked by security officials during the early 1990s. Outside KwaZulu-Natal, he was scarcely known, notwithstanding his status as a senior ANC office-holder. As Mbeki's deputy in the organisation and in the government, he could be counted upon to be loyal and skilful in all those managerial functions which Mbeki has performed for Mandela. That he has no significant public following outside his province does not seem to be viewed as a shortcoming; indeed, Mbeki may perceive this as an asset in a prospective subordinate. But in an ANC increasingly crowded with disrespectful young activists with no direct experience of the discipline or the inspiration of the struggle decades, age, status and track record will count for less and less. To maintain his authority, Mbeki will need showmanship and showmen (and show-women).

Apart from a concern for ethnic balancing (an important motive in Jacob Zuma's nomination), political criteria (at least, those which relate to personal popularity) seem to have less weight in Mbeki's preferred leadership appointments (or 'deployments', a favourite word in his political lexicon) in both government and party than technocratic or bureaucratic considerations. This is not necessarily a bad thing; personal popularity is no guarantee of effective executive performance. For example, Mrs Nkosazana Zuma may not be universally liked, but her administration of her health portfolio has already significantly and positively impacted upon public health. In the remainder of the Mandela presidency, any fresh cabinet appointments will be a crucial litmus of the kind of government that will rule South Africa in the future. If loyalty and personal connections seem to be more important than an established track record of executive competence and if new appointments are of relatively unknown people, then the chances of strong government will be diminished. To date, Mbeki's influenced cabinet appointments have a mixed record of success. He is generally credited with an imaginative and far-sighted choice of Trevor Manuel (a key UDF leader in the 1980s) as finance minister, but the selection of Sankie Mthembi-Mahanyele as the minister of housing seemed informed by narrower considerations of personal patronage, and her performance to date has been marred by allegations of nepotism. Not all post-1994 recruits to the government have been Mbeki acolytes, though. Bridget Mabandla, widely respected by the parliamentary caucus and a close associate of Cyril Ramaphosa, replaced Madikizela-Mandela in 1995 as deputy minister for arts, culture, science and technology. On the other hand, the man who replaced Tito Mboweni as labour minister, the comparatively unknown Membathisi Mdladlana, a former school principal, SACTU leader and COSATU parliamentary nominee, was perceived at the time of his appointment as a 'caretaker ... someone unlikely to rock the Mbeki boat'.[211]

Charismatic attributes of leadership can be acquired; they are not simply ingrained in particular personalities, and, of course, they are often the product of carefully fostered myths. Nelson Mandela's charisma is at least partly attributable to the legends created in his enforced absence from the political stage. Mbeki's lack of a comparatively heroic liberation biography, his relative youth, and his 'commoner' family status are factors which may inhibit any development of charismatic leadership attributes. But they do not represent unsurmountable obstacles to such a process. In the past Mbeki has been criticised for his uncomfortable oratorical manner. In fact he has become an increasingly relaxed public performer: his presentation of the ANC's testament to the Truth and Reconciliation Commission combined candour with warmth and included an improvised break into song which charmed his audience. It was by far the most impressive of the political party presentations to the Commission. Mbeki's speech at the adoption of the Constitution in 1996 was one of the most visionary and poetic public statements to have been delivered by an ANC leader in recent history, especially in its inclusive definition of Africanism, which represented one of the best statements about South African national identity to have been produced by any local politician.

Mbeki's attitudes about race are easy to misunderstand. His more recent statements decrying the economic selfishness of whites and their reluctance to commit themselves to a new patriotism can be interpreted as a cynical appeal to the social resentments which exist within the ANC's following. More fairly, they probably signify frustration at the absence of any evidence of a corresponding sense of Africanism among white political and business leaders. In a paper written a few months after the ANC's electoral victory, Mbeki argued that one of the ANC's main objectives should be to 'retain and increase our support among . . . the white middle strata'. To do this, he contended, 'it would also be important to deploy a fair number of white organisers to join this effort, to give reassurance that the new power is also based among the 'super-powerful' white minority. The message that the organisers must communicate to these communities is that the democratic transformation requires their skills and talents and therefore considers them a valuable national asset and a vital national component of the forces that we require to build a better life.'[212] Unlike the 'I am an African' prose, the language in this document is dispassionately analytical. It is directed at an internal audience, not the broader public, and it recognises the continuing salience of racial identity on political behaviour – but it also demonstrates a commitment to including white South Africans within a new patriotism. Such a commitment might be more obviously evident, though, if Mbeki included a few whites in his personal staff: this need not signify any weakened commitment to affirmative action. There are no whites either in the informal circle of advisers which since 1996 has met regularly to serve as a sounding-board for the deputy president's ideas.[213] However, Mbeki's vision of an African Renaissance in which an economically powerful South Africa can 'strike out on this new path' to nurture 'the rebirth of the continent' is defined in terms which are easy enough for white South African patriots to embrace, though, as we have noted in Chapter 8, not all Renaissance discourse is as socially inclusive.

What can be expected under a Mbeki presidency is that, in contrast to the Mandela era, there will be much less emphasis on placating white fears and, at least rhetorically, more evident concern with 'transformation' issues. A frequent Mbeki argument is that social harmony is impossible in a context in which 'poverty and prosperity continue to be defined in racial terms. If you want reconciliation between black and white, then you need to transform society.' In Mbeki's perception, however, not all opponents of transformation are white. In a speech introducing the parliamentary debate on his budget vote, he called for 'a halt to the abuse of freedom in the name of entitlement . . . especially by elements of the black elite' who 'hijack sacrifices . . . to satisfy a seemingly insatiable and morally unbound greed'.[214]

Thabo Mbeki seems to engender favourable perceptions amongst businessmen. Positive ratings in such exercises as the surveys undertaken by a Johannesburg business journal in 1996 and 1997[215] testify to the care and effort which he has invested in addressing the concerns of this constituency, both locally and abroad. He has been especially successful abroad, as Kaizer Nyatsumba noted in 1997: 'In Brussels . . . in Rome and in Amsterdam, not once in my 20 plus meetings with top political and business leaders did the question of Mbeki's suitability for the presidency come up, not once.'[216] In doing so, Mbeki has aroused sharp criticism from leading communists for his concept of a 'golden triangle' of business, labour and government, a term used in a 1997 ANC discussion paper, 'State and Social Transformation', widely believed to reflect Mbeki's thinking. But if some communists are critical of the ANC leadership's 'slide into a technocratic "class neutral" approach', Mbeki is not generally unpopular amongst the left. As the surveys cited above indicated, and more conclusively as a CASE survey also discovered in 1995, Mbeki enjoys the approval of many senior trade unionists, despite his early support for privatisation of state-owned corporations. Mbeki has a deft rhetorical capacity for steering a middle course between what he has dismissively called 'the paradigms of ideological dogma' – an aptitude which his supporters term 'pragmatism' and such detractors as the DP leader, Tony Leon, more unkindly describe as 'travelling on both sides of the road'. It may not enhance what the New York Times has disparagingly referred to as his 'trust factor',[217] but Mbeki's talent for compromise has animated an administration which can already claim to have gone some way towards the 'provision of a better life for all' while at the same time meeting, to quote Mbeki, the challenges of 'an historically unavoidable process of globalisation'. There are few developing countries which can make the same claim today.

Mbeki's policy pronouncements have been demonstrably consistent and they are informed by a deeper knowledge of the technicalities of economics and a better understanding of the wider world than are available to most of his colleagues. They form a fairly safe base from which to make predictions about the continuity under his presidency of the courses set during the Mandela administration. In a desperately unequal society, one which is still characterised by deep political conflict, Thabo Mbeki's qualities of political imagination, his sense of political balance and the survival skills honed in the difficult world of exile politics may well supply effective substitutes for the absent alchemy of Madiba magic.

NOTES

1. *The Star,* 7 November 1994 and 25 November 1994; *New Nation,* 9 December 1994.

2. ANC figures reported in *The Citizen,* 17 June 1991.

3. For the evolution of ANC economic programmes, see Nicoli Nattrass, 'Politics and economics in ANC policy', *African Affairs,* 93, 372, July 1994, pp. 343-360.

4. Jonathan Michie and Vishnu Padayachee, *The Political Economy of South Africa's Transition,* The Dryden Press, London, 1997, p. 46. See also Patrick Bond, 'The making of South Africa's macro-economic compromise' in Ernest Maganya and Rachel Houghton (eds.), *Transformation in South Africa? Policy Debates in the 1990s,* IFAA, Johannesburg, 1992.

5. African National Congress, *The Reconstruction and Development Programme: A Policy Framework,* Umanyano Publications, Johannesburg, 1994.

6. Pollsters in late 1994 found African ANC voters demonstrating patience with the new government and confidence that it would keep its promises. In a variety of policy-related questions respondents demonstrated a surprising degree of moderation in their expectations: for example, 61 per cent of the sample favoured smaller housing subsidies than those offered by the government so that more people could be helped sooner. See Lawrence Schlemmer, R.W. Johnson and Craig Charney, *South Africa: Findings of a Survey of Political and Social Attitudes in Post-Election South Africa,* December 1994, p. 20.

7. Of course, in certain respects, the state has become less socially autonomous and less powerful over the last decade, partly because of its rising indebtedness and also because of its democratisation, which has made public access to the state easier. Even so, South African government bureaucratic capacity compares favourably with most other African governments in the subcontinent for the extent of its social penetration, that is the range of citizenry affected by its actions, its extractive capacity – the social character of its taxation base – and its coercive authority. For the historical reasons for South Africa state strength see David Yudelman, *The Emergence of Modern South Africa,* David Philip, Cape Town, 1983, pp. 214-248.

8. In 1992, South Africa's total foreign debt was US$17 billion, 14.5 per cent of the country's GNP. Expressed as a proportion of GNP, only Mauritius and Botswana were relatively less indebted in Africa. Mozambique's foreign debt in 1992 was five times its GNP. See Pieter Esterhuysen, *Africa at a Glance,* Africa Institute, Pretoria, 1995, p. 51.

9. COSATU, 'A programme for the Alliance', *African Communist,* 146, 1997/8, p. 22.

10. Lynda Loxton, 'Job figures released', *The Star,* 15 October 1998.

11. COSATU, 'A programme for the Alliance', p. 22.

12. *Sunday Independent*, 20 April 1998.

13. African National Congress, *All Power to the People: Proposed Constitutional Amendments*, 50th National Congress, Marshalltown, Johannesburg, 1997.

14. 'Empowerment deal slowdown', *Sunday Times Business Times*, 18 October 1998.

15. See, for example, Thabo Mbeki's remarks on the racial representation of the South African Chamber of Business in Thabo Kobokoane, 'SACOB worried about restrictive labour laws', *Sunday Times Business Times*, 18 October 1998.

16. See the parliamentary register reproduced in *The Star*, 19 February 1998. The two richest members of parliament, Ben and Mary Turok, with shareholdings between them worth R1.5 million, are also amongst the most left-wing.

17. Jeremy Cronin and Blade Nzimande, 'ANC Thatcherites want a party of black bosses', *Mail & Guardian*, 10 October 1998.

18. Wally Mbhele, 'Mokaba tackles the SACP', *Mail & Guardian*, 3 October 1997.

19. Cyril Madlala, 'Mbeki's gauntlet', *The Star*, 12 September 1998.

20. Kerry Cullinan, 'Moosa raps COSATU for privatisation strike plan', *The Star*, 11 September 1998.

21. Ann Crotty, 'Ramaphosa calls for balanced labour law', *The Star*, 30 June 1998.

22. Kerry Cullinan, 'Hanekom defends property clause', *The Star*, 19 September 1998.

23. An IDASA–SABC–Markinor survey, *Opinion 99*, registered in October 1998 that 62.4 per cent of its respondents in rural settlements felt that the government was handling improving health services very well or fairly well compared to 50.5 per cent in metropolitan areas; 71.8 per cent of residents polled in the Eastern Cape responded to this question favourably compared to 35.8 per cent in the Western Cape. See Markinor, *Project Nyulo*, vol. 3, Table 86, p. 258.

24. Justin Arenstein, 'Big wheels', *Sunday Times*, 14 December 1997.

25. Jacquie Golding-Duffy, 'Plans to unseat the premier', *Mail & Guardian*, 28 June 1996.

26. Mark Gevisser, 'One Free State, one Lekota?', *Mail & Guardian*, 6 August 1996.

27. Wally Mbhele, 'The poison arrows are out for Ivy', *Mail & Guardian*, 7 August 1998.

28. For example, see Jovial Rantao, 'Motshekga in firing line', *The Star*, 15 July 1998, in which senior provincial ANC personalities, including two MECs, were alleged by 'Motshekga sympathizers' to be deliberately encouraging the premier to make mistakes by offering him bad advice.

29. Helen Taylor and Bob Mattes, *Political Parties and the Consolidation of Democracy in South Africa*, IDASA, Kutlwanong Democracy Centre, Pretoria, 29–30 September 1997; Marlene Roelfs, *Notes on Perceptions of Legitimacy of National and Provincial Government in the Western and Eastern Cape, KwaZulu-Natal and Gauteng*, paper presented at workshop on Democracy and Social Capital in Segmented Societies, Department of Political Studies, University of the Witwatersrand, Johannesburg, 9–12 October 1997.

30. Johan Olivier and Rose Ngwane, 'Marching to a different tune', *Indicator SA*, 1996.

31. All quotations in preceding paragraphs in this chapter are from African National Congress, *The Reconstruction and Development Programme*, Umanyano Publications, Johannesburg, 1994.

32. COSATU, NACTU and FEDSAL, *Social Equity and Job Creation, the Key to a Stable Future. Labour's Proposals on Growth, Development and Job Creation*, Johannesburg, 1 April 1996, p. 5.

33. Republic of South Africa, *White Paper on Reconstruction and Development: The Government's Strategy for Total Transformation*, Office of the President, Cape Town, 1994.

34. World Bank, *Development Report*, Oxford University Press, Oxford, 1997.

35. See especially Consolidated Business Movement, *Building a Winning Nation*, Ravan Press, Johannesburg, 1994. Also in this vein: J. Michael Cleverley, *South Africa's Obstacles: The RDP's Opportunities*, address by the counsellor for economic affairs, US Embassy, Pretoria, 22 June 1995.

36. 'Business: confused signals?', *RDP Monitor*, Stock Information Services, 1, 6, February 1995, p. 2.

37. Unless other sources are indicated, these statistics are taken from Republic of South Africa, *The Building has Begun! Government's Report to the Nation*, Government Communication and Information Service, Pretoria, February 1998.

38. Republic of South Africa, *The Foundation for a Better Life has been Laid: The Government's Mid-term Report to the Nation*, South African Communication Service, Pretoria, February 1997, p. 16.

39. Jim Day, 'Zuma's remarkable road to recovery', *Mail & Guardian*, 23 May 1997.

40. Derek Hanekom, 'Great progress in land redistribution', *Mail & Guardian*, 24 January 1998.

41. Official figures vary. The booklet cited above, published in February 1998, refers to 'close on 400,000 subsidised houses either completed or under construction'. In September 1998, Minister Sankie Mthembi-Mahanyele was quoted as claiming 596,059 houses built or under construction (Adele Lucas, 'Ministry gets realistic about housing targets', *Sunday Independent*, 27 September 1998), while the following month, a press report cited a ministry statement that 545,006 houses were completed or still being built (Nicole Turner, 'Housing plan is building momentum', *Reconstruct* in *Sunday Independent*, 25 October 1998). A figure of 235,000 houses completed is given in 'Whatever happened to the dream of low cost housing?', *Mail & Guardian*, 20 February 1998.

42. Clive Sawyer, 'Housing unit target of 1 million will be hard to achieve by 1999', *The Star*, 30 July 1998.

43. 'Asmal punts his achievements', *The Star*, 25 August 1998.

44. Melanie-Ann Feris, 'Historic watershed in the lives of many', *The Star*, 8 October 1997.

45. The South African Institute of Race Relations *Annual Surveys* for the late 1950s and early 1960s suggest an annual rate of 'sub-economic' housing construction for Africans, much of it financed through private sector loans to the government, of between 25,000 and 35,000 a year. This level was only beginning to be revived in the late 1980s after a long period in which the state built or financed very small numbers of houses for Africans. See also John Kane-Berman, *Soweto: Black Revolt, White Reaction*, Ravan Press, Johannesburg, 1978, pp. 58–61.

46. '2.6-m housing units needed', *The Star*, 24 September 1998.

47. Richard Abel, *Politics by Other Means: Law in the Struggle against Apartheid*, Routledge, London, 1995, p. 401.

48. Pieter Esterhuysen, *Africa A–Z: Continental and Country Profiles*, Africa Institute, Pretoria, 1998, p. 52.

49. Jim Day, 'Zuma's remarkable road to recovery', *Mail & Guardian*, 23 May 1997. South African infant mortality remains higher than Botswana's, for instance, and that of

several other much poorer African countries.

50. David Robbins, 'Making our health service better for all', *The Star*, 20 December 1998.

51. Graham McIntosh, President of the KwaZulu-Natal Agricultural Union, interviewed in the *Helen Suzman Foundation KwaZulu-Natal Briefing*, September 1998, p. 19; Mbongeni Ngubeni, 'Understanding and dealing with the killings on farms', *The Star*, 9 October 1998.

52. The statistic refers to the King Edward Hospital in Durban. See Ann Eveleth, 'Cash is the only cure for ailing hospitals', *Mail & Guardian*, 6 February 1998.

53. Kader Asmal, 'We must treat our water, that life-giving essence, as if we found ourselves on a spaceship', *Sunday Independent*, 18 May 1997.

54. Department of Water Affairs and Forestry, *Evaluation of the Community Water Supply and Sanitation Programme*, Workshop Document, Mvula Trust, Pretoria, November 1997.

55. Ned Breslin, 'There's a hole in South Africa's water bucket', *Reconstruct* in *Sunday Independent*, 4 October 1998.

56. A good example of the advantages of working through large-scale organisations would be the case of ISCOR. An ISCOR subsidiary, Balaton Housing, has developed a steel building system which owners can easily erect for themselves. Some 4000 of these houses were built at Phomolong for R7000 a structure, leaving the rest of the subsidy for infrastructure: roads, water and sewerage. Advertisement: 'Iscor: Building the Nation', *Reader's Digest*, June 1996.

57. Ryan Cresswell, 'Unique housing scheme a dream come true for women', *The Star*, 25 February 1998.

58. For details of an Ennerdale women's group, see Bongiwe Mlangeni, 'Stokvel makes dreams of own houses a reality', *The Star*, 20 November 1995; for obstructive official attitudes with respect to a community self-help project in Sivukile, Mpumalanga, see Susan Miller, 'Individuals pull together to uplift community', *The Star*, 6 February 1996.

59. Celean Jacobson, 'This is the house Winnie's building', *Sunday Times*, 15 December 1996.

60. Alan Lipman, 'Apartheid ends, but they're still put in little boxes, little boxes all the same', *Sunday Independent*, 3 March 1996.

61. For details of such schemes in Newtown, Johannesburg, and in Payne Park, Germiston, see Hopewell Radebe, 'Rental home projects for low wage earners', *The Star*, 5 October 1998 and Adele Shevel, 'Germiston leads way in housing project', *The Star*, 23 July 1998.

62. Between 1989 and 1998 the matriculation repeater rate (the proportion of students who re-enrolled for a second year in Standard 10) rose from 19 per cent to 40 per cent. See Jacqui Reeves, 'Classroom failures strain education budget', *The Star*, 1 September 1998.

63. The very small proportion of women among the elected councillors, 18.75 per cent, suggests that gender prejudices inhibit political parties from effectively deploying all the potentially competent representatives among their memberships. The ANC did ensure that every second candidate on its PR list was female but very few women were elected in the wards.

64. Community Elections Evaluation Group, *The End of the Beginning: An Evaluation of the November 1995 South African Local Government Elections*, CEEG, Johannesburg, July

1996, p. 60. The proportion of registered electors who voted was higher, about 65 per cent.

65. *Ibid*, p. 179.

66. Comparisons with other African countries suggest a more encouraging perspective: for example, in Zambia the first post-democratisation local elections elicited a voter turn-out of below 10 per cent (Siegmar Schmidt, 'Is small beautiful?' in Wilhelm Hofmeister and Ingo Scholz (eds.), *Traditional and Contemporary Forms of Local Participation and Self-Government in Africa*, Konrad-Adenauer-Stiftung, Johannesburg, 1997, p. 46).

67. See, for example, Lawrence Schlemmer, 'Birth of democracy', *Indicator SA*, 11, 3, Winter 1994, p. 19.

68. For an example of the tensions arising from such an incident in Johannesburg's EMSS where a SANCO branch secretary was actually placed on the list, only to be then informed that he had 'resigned' in favour of an ANC official, see Charmeela Bhagowat, 'Tensions between ANC and civics', *The Star*, 20 February 1995.

69. Adrian Hadland, 'The ANC just lost the poll, but its leaders are grinning from ear to ear', *Sunday Independent*, 2 June 1996.

70. For details of other incidents see Graeme Gotz, 'Battles ahead? Conflict in local government elections', *Election Watch Briefing Document 10*, Centre for Policy Studies, 1995, pp. 5–7.

71. HSRC and Department of Political Studies, University of the Witwatersrand, *Markdata Omnibus Survey on Local Government*, September 1995; reports held in the Department of Political Studies, University of the Witwatersrand. All subsequent references to survey evidence in this chapter refer to this data set.

72. African National Congress, *Local Government Elections: Campaign Manual*, Voter Education and Training Unit, Johannesburg, 1995, p. 17.

73. The Department of Political Studies, University of the Witwatersrand–HSRC Local Government Research Project employed 20 fieldworkers in the months before the election to monitor events. Much of the information in this chapter is drawn from their unpublished reports held in the Political Studies Department at Wits.

74. Bongiwe Mlangeni, 'Action needed to put Masakhane and RDP on track', *The Star*, 27 September 1995.

75. Jane Carruthers, *Sandton: The Making of a Town*, Clet Books, Rivonia, 1993.

76. For example, in 1996 EMSS councillors, opposed by the DP, voted for a 94 per cent increase in allowances, bringing their monthly remuneration to R5484 in the case of ordinary councillors and over R15,000 (including R3895 travel expenses) for executive members (*The Star*, 29 November 1998). Steyn Commission proposals suggest that executive members of the top tier of larger municipalities should be paid R10,893 a month (*The Star*, 24 December 1996). The proposals were adopted in mid-1997 and councillors earning more than the recommended rates had their salaries frozen. But non-elected officials are also often extremely well paid. The nine most senior council managers in Johannesburg earned packages worth between R27,000 and R30,000 in 1996 (*The Star*, 20 August 1996).

77. 'Do you know your mayor? Not many do', *The Star*, 7 November 1996.

78. 'SAMWU rejects Nelspruit's muddy waters', *The Star*, 22 April 1997.

79. For details, see Republic of South Africa, *White Paper on Local Government* in *Government Gazette*, no. 18739, 18 March 1998; Republic of South Africa, *Local*

Government: Municipal Structures Bill, B68–98.

80. NP spokesperson Hans Eybers quoted in 'Khayalami in megacity move', *The Star*, 20 October 1998.

81. Frances Kendall, 'We will pay more and get less', *The Star*, 13 September 1997.

82. Phillip Frankel, Stephen Louw and Simon Stacey, *Governmental Performance and Capacity: Transitional Local Authorities in Mpumalanga*, Department of Political Studies, University of the Witwatersrand, and HSRC External Projects Programme, April 1997.

83. *Ibid*, p. 241.

84. IDASA Public Opinion Service, *POS Reports*, no. 3, February 1996, 'Parliamentary ethics and government corruption: playing with public trust'.

85. *Transparency International Corruption Perception Index*, 1997, press release, Johannesburg, 31 July 1997. This agency collates the results of at least four surveys of perceptions with respect to 52 countries so as to construct a ranking. South Africa's score out of 10.00 slipped from 5.68 to 4.95 between 1996 and 1997, locating it at 33rd position. Its 1998 score, published by TI in an advertisement in *Reconstruct*, a supplement to the *Sunday Independent* (1 November 1998), had improved slightly, to 5.2, earning it a 32nd position on the index.

86. Victor Levine, *Political Corruption: The Ghana Case*, Stanford University Press, Stanford, 1975.

87. Robert C. Brooks. 'The nature of political corruption' in Arnold J. Heidenheimer (ed.), *Political Corruption: Readings in Comparative Analysis*, Holt, Reinhart and Winston, New York, 1970.

88. Robert Klitgaard, *Controlling Corruption*, University of California Press, Berkeley, 1988, p. 20.

89. *The Economist*, 21 August 1996.

90. Crawford Young and Thomas Turner, *The Rise and the Decline of the Zairean State*, University of Wisconsin Press, Madison, 1985, pp. 401–402.

91. See Joseph Nye, 'Corruption and political development: a political cost-benefit analysis', *American Political Science Review*, 56, 1967, and Nathaniel Leff, 'Economic development through corruption' in Heidenheimer, *Political Corruption*.

92. M. McMullen, 'A theory of corruption', *Sociological Review*, 1961, p. 184.

93. Donatella Della Porta and Yves Meny (eds.), *Democracy and Corruption in Europe*, Pinter, London, 1997.

94. Anthony Minaar, Ian Liebenberg and Charl Schutte, *The Hidden Hand: Covert Operations in South Africa*, HSRC, Pretoria, 1994, p. 321.

95. R. Hengeveld and J. Rodenburg, *Embargo: Apartheid's Oil Secrets Revealed*, Shipping Research Bureau, Amsterdam University Press, Amsterdam, 1995.

96. Republic of South Africa, *Commission of Inquiry into Development Aid*, Pretoria, RP 73/1992.

97. Republic of South Africa, *Verslag van die Kommissie van Ondersoek na die 1980 Onluste en beweerde Wanbestuur in KwaNdebele*, Pretoria, RP 137/1993.

98. Gerhard Maré and Georgina Hamilton, *An Appetite for Power: Buthelezi's Inkatha and the Politics of 'Loyal Resistance'*, Ravan Press, Johannesburg, 1987, p. 91.

99. Themba Sepotokele, 'Claims of housing corruption', *The Star*, 31 December 1997.

100. Media and Marketing Research, *Sowetan Crime Survey: Presentation of Crime Findings*, Johannesburg, January 1996, p. 12.

101. Jovial Rantao, 'Judge's help sought in uncovering welfare scams', *The Star*, 11 March 1998.

102. Mzilikazi wa Afrika, 'Legal beagles to probe R30m fraud', *Mail & Guardian*, 20 March 1998.

103. Jovial Rantao, 'Enormous fraud found in food programmes', *The Star*, 4 June 1998.

104. Adrian Hadland, 'Heath unit makes big inroads on fraud', *The Star*, 22 August 1998; 'Corruption shrinking budgets', *The Star*, 28 August 1998.

105. Jovial Rantao, 'Job creation becomes fraud creation', *The Star*, 12 August 1997.

106. Anthony Johnson, 'Midweek politics', *Cape Times*, 23 July 1997.

107. Justin Arenstein, 'Sacked game parks boss lashes Phosa over Berlin Wall', *Sunday Times*, 18 October 1998.

108. Andy Duffy, 'Mokaba's plastic shopping spree', *Mail & Guardian*, 24 April 1998.

109. A Markdata survey in mid-1996 indicated ANC support at 52.9 per cent, whereas a Markinor mock ballot in May 1996 registered 63 per cent in favour of the ANC (Susan Booysen, 'ANC far ahead in the 1996 race', *The Star*, 11 February 1997). An IDASA poll conducted in June 1998 suggested that 52.5 voters would support the ANC (Donwald Pressly, 'Survey shows solid support for the ANC', *The Star*, 7 October 1998). An SABC–IDASA–Markinor survey found in October 1998 that 51.4 per cent of its sample would support the ANC 'if there were an election tomorrow', with 14.2 per cent indicating that it was 'not likely' they would vote and a further 6 per cent suggesting it was uncertain (Tables 146 and 178, Markinor, *Project Nyulo*, vol. 1, October 1998).

110. Parks Mankahlana, 'Angola shows us how valuable ANC–IFP unity would be to SA', *Sunday Independent*, 11 January 1998.

111. Blade Nzimande, 'ANC–Inkatha alliance far-fetched', *New Nation*, 26 July 1996.

112. Jeremy Cronin, 'Base ANC–IFP merger on honesty, not fiction', *Mail & Guardian*, 13 February 1998.

113. Ruth Rabinowitz, 'ANC and IFP not likely to merge soon', *The Star*, 18 December 1997; M.J. Bhengu, 'Loose talk about a national alliance is irresponsible', *Natal Mercury*, 9 December 1997.

114. The phrases are from *Speech by ANC Deputy President Thabo Mbeki to the annual conference of the IFP, 18 July 1998*, ANC Department of Information and Publicity, Marshalltown, 1998, p. 6.

115. Lester Venter, *When Mandela Goes: The Coming of South Africa's Second Revolution*, Doubleday, Johannesburg, 1997.

116. The ANC does not publish national membership statistics, but provincial spokesmen have admitted that their memberships have fallen from 120,000 in 1994 to 44,000 in Gauteng and from 33,000 paid-up members in the Western Cape in 1996 to 22,000 in late 1997 (Marco Granelli, 'ANC draws up battle plan to crush all forces', *The Star*, 30 March 1998; 'Rassool chosen to lead ANC in Western Cape', *The Star*, 20 April 1998).

117. A. Mazrui and G. Engholm, 'The tensions of crossing the floor' in Ali Mazrui (ed.), *Violence and Thought: Essays in Social Tensions in Africa*, Heinemann, London, 1969.

118. All the above quotations are from 'The state, property relations and social transformation', *Umrabulo*, 5, Department of Political Education and Training, African National Congress, Marshalltown, 1998, pp. 38–60.

119. Jovial Rantao, 'ANC calls Judge de Villiers a dinosaur', *The Star*, 19 June 1998.

120. Prakash Naidoo, 'Plot to foil health reforms', *Sunday Independent*, 18 October 1998.

121. Marco Granelli, 'ANC draws up battle plan to crush all forces', *The Star*, 30 March 1998.

122. *Political Report of the President, Nelson Mandela, to the 50th National Conference of the African National Congress: Mafikeng, December 16, 1997*, Mathibe Printing and Publishing, Johannesburg, pp. 12–18.

123. Robert Putnam, *Making Democracy Work: Civic Traditions in Modern Italy*, Princeton University Press, Princeton, New Jersey, 1993.

124. Gumisae Mutume, 'Too few NGOs in South Africa involved in development', *The Star*, 22 October 1996.

125. Glenda Daniels, 'Foreign funding likely to dry up', *The Star*, 28 September 1994.

126. Rod Amner, 'The NGO funding drought', *The Star*, 4 September 1995.

127. R.W. Johnson, 'Destroying South Africa's democracy', *The National Interest*, Fall 1998, p. 25.

128. Dietrich Rueschemeyer, Evelyne Huber Stephens and John D. Stephens, *Capitalist Development and Democracy*, Polity Press, Oxford, 1992, p. 61.

129. Wilmot James and Moira Levy (eds.), *Pulse: Passages in Democracy-Building: Assessing South Africa's Transition*, IDASA, Cape Town, 1998, p. 93.

130. SABC–IDASA–Markinor, *Opinion 99, Project Nyulo*, vol. 1, Table 25, Markinor, Johannesburg, October 1998. The 1994 figure is from R.W. Johnson and Lawrence Schlemmer, *Launching Democracy: The First Open Election, April 1994*, Yale University Press, New Haven, p. 261. The disparity between the two survey findings may be attributable partly to the slightly less assertive wording employed in the question posed in 1994, 'would not allow', as opposed to 'might take part in action', though the apparent growth in tolerance does correlate with other surveys.

131. Adam Habib and Rupert Taylor, 'No real opposition on the horizon', *The Star*, 9 November 1998.

132. For a sampling, see Libby Husemeyer, *Watchdogs or Hypocrites: The Amazing Debate on South African Liberals and Liberalism*, Friedrich-Naumann-Stiftung, Johannesburg, 1997.

133. Colin Bundy, 'Survival and resistance: township organisations and non-violent direct action in twentieth-century South Africa' in Glenn Adler and Jonny Steinberg (eds.), *From Comrades to Citizens*, Macmillan, London, 1998.

134. Kevin French, *James Mpanza and the Sofasonke Movement*, MA dissertation, Department of Political Studies, University of the Witwatersrand, 1984; A.W. Stadler, 'Birds in the cornfield: squatter movements in Johannesburg, 1944–1947', *Journal of Southern African Studies*, 6, 1, 1979.

135. *Mail & Guardian*, 19 September 1997.

136. Marina Ottaway, 'African democratisation and the Leninist option', *Journal of Modern African Studies*, 35, 1, 1997, p. 11.

137. Ben Jacobs, 'SANCO: heading for disaster', *Work in Progress*, 86, 1992.

138. Mzwanele Mayekiso, 'Institutions that themselves need to be watched over: a review of recent writings on the civic movement', *Urban Forum*, 41, 1994.

139. Moses Mayekiso, interviewed in *Reconstruct*, supplement to *Work in Progress*, June 1992.

140. Lechesa Tsenoli, interview, *Development and Democracy*, 8, 1994.

141. Adrian Hadland, 'SANCO leader warns ANC that it cannot rest on its laurels', *Sunday Independent*, 17 November 1996.

142. *Umthunywa*, 3, June 1995.

143. 'Why SANCO changed its tune', *New Nation*, 20 March 1997.

144. Amrit Manga, 'ANC Lekgotla: does it point the way forward?', *New Nation*, 24 January 1997.

145. Jeremy Seekings, 'SANCO: strategic dilemmas in a democratic South Africa', *Transformation*, 34, 1997, p. 16.

146. David Robbins, 'SANCO's radical alternative', *The Star*, 12 July 1995.

147. Newton Kanhema, 'Row over bond freeze', *Sunday Star*, 26 July 1992.

148. Kimberley Lanegran, 'South Africa's civic association movement: ANC's ally or society's watchdog?', *African Studies Review*, 38, 2, September 1995.

149. Sandi Mgidlana, 'SANCO hits back', *New Nation*, 19 July 1996.

150. William Mervin Gumede, 'SANCO marches to a business drum', *The Star*, 28 December 1996.

151. Adrian Hadland, 'SANCO leader warns ANC that it cannot rest on its laurels', *Sunday Independent*, 17 November 1996.

152. SANCO, *Strategies and Policies for Local Economic Development in the New South Africa*, Johannesburg, March 1995.

153. *Umthunywa*, 3 June 1995.

154. Stefaans Brummer, 'Corruption probe into SANCO donations', *Mail & Guardian*, 1 September 1995.

155. William Mervin Gumede, 'SANCO's Gauteng province rallies around expelled Mayekiso', *Sunday Independent*, 24 August 1997.

156. National Interim Civic Committee, *Financial Statement*, October 1991–June 1992.

157. Pule Molebeledi, 'Mayor quits to join SANCO', *New Nation*, 24 January 1997.

158. Deon Delport, 'SANCO wants people to be proud informers', *The Star*, 3 March 1997.

159. *Reconstruct*, June 1992.

160. Mzwanele Mayekiso, 'SANCO and politics: then and now', *New Nation*, 13 December 1996.

161. William Mervin Gumede, 'ANC alliance suffers first split as Transkei civics quit', *Sunday Independent*, 19 October 1997.

162. Farouk Chotia, 'Clash over role of traditional leaders', *Mail & Guardian*, 18 November 1994.

163. 'The role of civics', *Mayibuye*, December 1960, p. 31.

164. 'SANCO branch soon from Queenstown central', *The Representative*, 19 June 1998.

165. Justine Lucas, 'Space, domesticity and people's power: civic organisation in Alexandra in the 1990s', *African Studies*, 54, 1, 1995, p. 102.

166. Mcebisi Ndletyana, *Changing Role of Civic Organisations from the Apartheid to the Post-Apartheid Era. A Case Study of the Alexandra Civic Organisation*, Department of Political Studies, University of the Witwatersrand, MA dissertation, 1998, pp. 64–68.

167. Caroline White, 'Democratic societies? Voluntary association and democratic culture in a South African township', *Transformation*, 36, 1998.

168. Abbey Mokoe, 'Police probe claim that R600 000 disappeared from Soweto civic's coffers', *The Star*, 8 July 1996.

169. Phillip Frankel, Steven Louw and Simon Stacey, *Governmental Performance and*

Capacity: Transitional Local Authorities in Mpumalanga, Department of Political Studies, University of the Witwatersrand, and the HSRC, April 1997, p. 257.

170. Middelburg Observer, 11 September 1998. The Wits researchers suggest that action against defaulters enjoys quite considerable community sanction, partly because the payment boycotts of the 1980s had always been locally 'goal-oriented' and 'as a result, Middelburg's black residents' were 'educated to understand non-payment as an always temporary exception to the rule' (Frankel, Louw and Stacey, Governmental Performance, p. 244). It may be the case that SANCO's following is concentrated amongst older residents of the city with experiences dating from this period, whereas the new committee may draw its support from relative newcomers to the town.

171. Isaac Makgabutlane, 'SANCO consults ratepayers body', Springs African Reporter, 28 August 1998.

172. Paul Kirk, 'Bitter feud over priest's grave', The Star, 3 January 1998.

173. For a stokvel housing initiative in Vosloorus, East Rand, see Bongiwe Mlangeni, 'Building bigger for less without the government subsidy', The Star, 24 March 1997. In Mhinga, Northern Province, and in Orange Farm, near Johannesburg, see William Mervin Gumede, 'They're helping themselves to houses', The Star, 20 July 1996. For reference to the Tswaranang Stokvel Group, Soweto, which built 40 houses in 1996, see Bongiwe Mlangeni, 'Housing for all still a dream', The Star, 23 December 1996.

174. Peter Mosang, Social Capital, Democracy and Development in Galeshewe Township, Kimberley, BA Honours dissertation, Department of Political Studies, University of the Witwatersrand, 1997.

175. Debates of the National House of Assembly, 10 June 1997, p. 3654.

176. 'The deputy president's address to the Corporate Council Summit, Chantilly, Virginia, April 1997' in Konrad-Adenauer-Stiftung, Occasional Papers: The African Renaissance, Johannesburg, May 1998.

177. Political Report of the President, Nelson Mandela, to the 50th National Conference of the African National Congress, Mafikeng, 16 December 1997, pp. 34 37.

178. Nthobi Moahloli (general manager, Corporate Affairs, Engen Limited), 'Afrika-tourism: using tourism to let Africans know Africa', Address to the African Renaissance Conference, Johannesburg, 28 September 1998.

179. Mondli Makhanya, 'Time to recolonise bits of Africa', The Star, 28 August 1998.

180. Jordan K. Ngubane, Ushaba: A Zulu Umlando, Three Continents Press, Washington, 1975.

181. Jabu Sindane, Democracy in African Societies and Ubuntu, HSRC, Centre for Constitutional Analysis, Pretoria, n.d., p. 8.

182. Yvonne Mokgoro, 'Ubuntu and the law in Africa', Konrad-Adenauer-Stiftung, Occasional Papers: The African Renaissance, Johannesburg, May 1998, p. 52.

183. Frank Nxumalo, 'Asmal taps into safe water', The Star, 5 May 1997.

184. Quotations from Robert W. July, An African Voice: The Role of the Humanities in African Independence, Duke University Press, Durham, 1987, pp. 222–223.

185. William Makgoba, 'A basis for the African Renaissance', African Renaissance Conference, 28–29 September 1998.

186. Kwesi Kwaa Prah, 'Who is an African?', African Renaissance Conference, 28–29 September 1998.

187. Cited on the letters page, Mail & Guardian, 11 September 1998, p. 26.

188. Nnamdi Azikiwe, *Renascent Africa*, Negro University Press, New York, 1969.

189. Leonard Barnes, *African Renaissance*, Victor Gollancz, London, 1969.

190. Thoahlane, *Black Renaissance: Papers from the Black Renaissance Convention*, Ravan Press, Johannesburg, 1974, pp. 7–8.

191. John Battersby, 'Mbeki the philosopher soars above the turmoil of Africa', *Sunday Independent*, 16 August 1998.

192. John Spira, 'Boom time for black business', *Sunday Independent*, 21 June 1998.

193. 'Public servants won't be ousted, says minister', *The Star*, 14 June 1998.

194. Pila Rulashe, 'Booming black middle class transforming insurance', *Sunday Independent*, 18 May 1998.

195. Republic of Uganda, Address by HE Yoweri Kaguta Museveni, *Why Africa Matters*, Buenos Aires University, 1 November 1994, p. 10.

196. Statement of Deputy President Thabo Mbeki at the African Renaissance Conference, Johannesburg, 28 September 1998, p. 2.

197. Joe Teffo, 'An African Renaissance: could it be realized?', *Woord en Daad*, 37, 361, Spring 1997.

198. Colin Bundy, 'Introduction', Govan Mbeki, *Learning from Robben Island*, David Philip, Cape Town, 1991, p. ix.

199. Kaizer Nyatsumba, 'The humble Mbeki', *The Star*, 3 September 1993.

200. Shaun Johnson, 'Pipe aroma marks Thabo territory', *The Star*, 10 June 1994.

201. Charlene Smith, 'Two faces of the struggle', *Saturday Star*, 20 June 1998.

202. Thabo Mbeki, 'The historical injustice', in African National Congress, *Selected Writings on the Freedom Charter*, Sechaba Commemorative Publications, London, 1985, p. 48.

203. In Ramaphosa's case, apparently, despite efforts by Mbeki to discourage his ascent in business. Lizeka Mda writes that 'the same Mbeki is reported to have summoned a prominent member of the National Empowerment Consortium in 1996 to impress upon that member that under no circumstances should Cyril Ramaphosa . . . be allowed to take control of Johnnic's media assets, largely represented by Times Media Limited. Today Ramaphosa is chair of both Johnnic and TML' (Lizeka Mda, 'A short leap to dictatorship', *Mail & Guardian*, 27 March 1998).

204. Justice Malala, 'Lasting enigma of South African politics', *The Star*, 17 March 1997.

205. According to one apparently well-informed authority, Mbeki 'was the first of the senior leadership to discern that the model the ANC had constructed for the RDP was seriously, probably fatally flawed. He believed the RDP might lead his countrymen up a blind alley of expectations which could not be met and might therefore give the government cause for serious regret. Other counsels prevailed and Mbeki's thumbs-down prior to the tabling of the White Paper was disregarded, to his dismay.' See Ingrid Uys, 'The compelling future of Thabo Mbeki', *Millennium Magazine*, May 1996, p. 34.

206. 'Mbeki's blues', *Southern African Report*, August 1998, p. 3.

207. *Sunday Times*, 7 May 1995

208. Kaizer Nyatsumba, 'Mbeki is passing the acid test', *The Star*, 11 June 1997.

209. Kaizer Nyatsumba, 'Rank and file flex their muscles', *The Star*, 19 February 1997.

210. Mondli Makhanya, 'Mbeki: ruthless politician or inefficient successor to Mandela?', *The Star*, 27 August 1996.

211. Andy Duffy, 'A caretaker in the cabinet', *Mail & Guardian*, 17 July 1998.

212. *From Resistance to Reconstruction. Tasks of the ANC in the New Epoch of the Democratic Transformation. Unmandated reflections*, 9 August 1994, p. 18.

213. Marion Edmunds, 'Who's who in Mbeki's private think-tank', *Mail & Guardian*, 19 July 1996. Participants listed in this report included cabinet members Joe Modise and Sydney Mufamadi as well as the deputy foreign affairs minister, Aziz Pahad; COSATU general secretary, Sam Shilowa; *City Press* editor, Khulu Sibiya; Eric Molobi of the Kagiso Trust; president of the South African Olympic Committee, Sam Ramsamy; Linda Zama, a Durban lawyer; and Ann Letsebe, then a university social work lecturer; the five directors of an investment syndicate, African Renaissance Holdings; the rector of MEDUNSA, Ephraim Mokgokong; Vincent Maphai of the HSRC; Wally Serote, poet and MP; chairman of the SABC board, Professor Paulus Zulu; and SACP general secretary, Charles Ngakula.

214. Jovial Rantao, 'Blacks must create own destiny, says Mbeki', *The Star*, 4 June 1998.

215. Ray Wood, 'South Africa's leaders rate Mbeki', *Professional Management Review*, July 1966, pp. 20–21; 'Fifty-one leaders rate Mbeki highly as future President', *Professional Management Review*, December 1997, pp. 8–10.

216. Kaizer Nyatsumba, 'Mbeki is passing the acid test', *The Star*, 11 June 1997.

217. *New York Times*, 23 July 1996.

INDEX